THEMATIC UNIT
Chocolate

Written by Janna Reed

with contributions by Mary Ellen Sterling

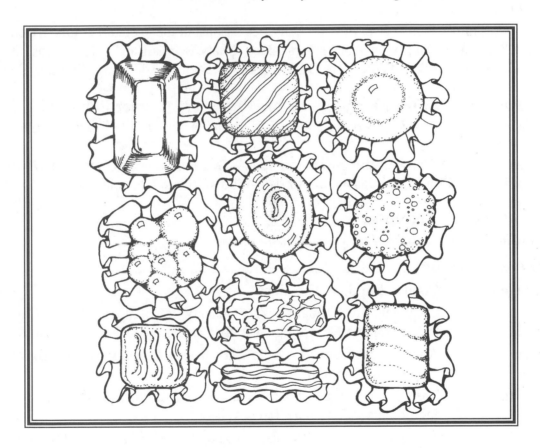

Teacher Created Materials, Inc.
6421 Industry Way
Westminster, CA 92683
www.teachercreated.com
ISBN-1-55734-239-3
©*1994 Teacher Created Materials, Inc.*
Reprinted, 1999
Made in U.S.A.

Illustrated by
Sue Fullam
Chris Perry

Edited by
Karen J. Goldfluss

Cover Art by
Blanca Apodaca LaBounty

Table of Contents

Introduction

Chocolate contains a captivating, whole language, thematic unit which gives students both a real and imaginary look at one of the world's most irresistible confections. Its 80 pages are filled with a wide variety of lesson ideas and reproducible pages designed for use with intermediate children. This literature-based thematic unit has at its core, three high-quality children's literature selections: *The Chocolate Touch, Charlie and the Chocolate Factory,* and *Vanilla, Chocolate, & Strawberry.* For each of these books, activities are included which set the stage for reading, encourage the enjoyment of the book, and extend the concepts gained. In addition, the theme is connected to the curriculum with activities in language arts, math, science, social studies, art, and life skills. Many of the activities are additional time savers for the busy teacher. Highlighting this complete teacher resource is a culminating activity. These activities allow students to synthesize and apply the knowledge beyond the classroom.

This thematic unit includes the following:

☐ **Literature selections**—summaries of three children's books with related lessons (complete with reproducible pages) that cross the curriculum

☐ **Planning guides**—suggestions for sequencing lessons each day of the unit

☐ **Writing ideas**—poetry and writing suggestions for writing across the curriculum

☐ **Curriculum connections**—activities in language arts, math, science, social studies, art, and life skills

☐ **Group projects**—activities to foster cooperative learning

☐ **Bulletin board ideas**—suggestions and plans for student-created and /or interactive bulletin boards

☐ **Culminating activities**—ideas which require students to synthesize their learning by engaging in an activity that can be shared by others

☐ **A bibliography**—a list suggesting additional literature books on the theme

> To keep this valuable resource intact so it can be used year after year, you may wish to punch holes in the pages and store them in a three-ring binder.

Introduction *(cont.)*

Why Whole Language?

A whole language approach involves children using all modes of communication: reading, writing, listening, observing, illustrating, and speaking. Communication skills are integrated into lessons which emphasize the whole of language rather than isolating its parts. A child reads, writes (spelling appropriately for his/her level), speaks, listens, and thinks in response to a literature experience introduced by the teacher. In this way language skills grow naturally, stimulated by involvement and interest in the topic at hand.

Why Thematic Planning?

One useful tool for implementing an integrated whole language program is thematic planning. By choosing a theme with corresponding literature selections for a unit of study, a teacher can plan activities throughout the day that lead to cohesive, in-depth study of the topic. Students practice and apply their skills in meaningful contexts. Consequently, they tend to learn and retain more. Both teachers and students are freed from a day that is broken into unrelated segments of isolated drill and practice.

Why Cooperative Learning?

In addition to academic skills and content, students need to learn social skills. No longer can this area of development be taken for granted. Students must learn to work cooperatively in groups in order to function well in modern society. Group activities should be a regular part of school life, and teachers should consciously include social objectives as well as academic objectives in their planning. The teacher should clarify and monitor the qualities of good group interaction just as he/she would clarify and monitor the academic goals of a project.

The Chocolate Touch

by Patrick Skene Catling

Summary

John Midas loves chocolate more than anything else in the world. After trading an old coin he finds for a box of chocolates, strange things begin happening. After John bites into the only piece of chocolate in the box, everything tastes like chocolate. In the events which follow, John discovers that his chocolate touch is a bit more than he can handle. Finally, when his mother turns to chocolate from his kiss, John is ready for help.

The outline below is a suggested plan for using the various activities that are presented in this unit. You should adapt these to fit your own classroom situation.

Sample Plan

Lesson I

- Read *King Midas and the Golden Touch*. Begin reading *The Chocolate Touch*.
- Write letters to chocolate manufacturing companies (page 5).
- Assign chocolate consumption survey (page 68).

Lesson II

- Continue reading *The Chocolate Touch*.
- Discuss character similarities (page 6).
- Create stories in cooperative groups (pages 44-46).
- Write imaginative book reports (pages 9-10).

Lesson III

- Finish reading *The Chocolate Touch*. Complete fishing and clothing industry activities (pages 11-12).
- Experiment with candy-covered chocolate (page 51).
- Play Chocolate Checkers game (pages 13-15).
- Discuss results of chocolate consumption survey (page 68).

Lesson IV

- Write poems about chocolate (pages 41-42).
- Enjoy chocolate food snacks (pages 69-70).
- Complete logic puzzle (page 47).
- Determine probabilities (page 16).
- Overview of Activities

Overview of Activities

Setting the Stage

1. Encourage students to become actively involved in the early stages of unit planning by writing letters to manufacturers requesting information about their chocolate products. Many companies are willing to send information about their products. (See page 80 for a list of addresses for some companies that produce products in which chocolate is the chief ingredient.) Ask students to share the information they receive.

Overview of Activities *(cont.)*

Setting the Stage *(cont.)*

2. Prepare a center in the classroom with resources about chocolate. Ask students to contribute wrappers from chocolate candies which can be used for some of the activities in the unit.

3. Set up some of the bulletin boards suggested on page 74. Display students' work and/or use the bulletin boards as active learning tools throughout the unit.

4. The story of King Midas is familiar to many students. Ask students if they know what the phrase "the Midas touch" means. Read aloud *King Midas and the Golden Touch* by Freya Littledale (Scholastic, Inc., 1989). If possible, make available the audio cassette, *The Golden Touch: A Greek Myth* (adapted by Michelle Baron, Alchemy Communications, 1987) for students to listen to at a classroom center. Explain to students that as they read *The Chocolate Touch*, they should look for ways in which the two stories parallel each other.

Enjoying the Book

1. Read chapters one and two of *The Chocolate Touch*. Ask students the following questions: How did John feel about candy? Would he share? What do you think is happening to him? Why is too much candy not good for John? (He eats too much of it and doesn't get enough nutrients from other foods.) Allow students to discuss their responses in small groups. Then regroup for a class discussion.

2. Finish reading *The Chocolate Touch*. Discuss the sequence of events that occur as a result of John's chocolate touch. Ask students to imagine some of the complications or unexpected changes that might result in a city "touched by chocolate." Have students complete the activity on page 11 and "The Dress Mess" activity on page 12.

3. Have students complete the Character Similarity on page 8 to compare the values, actions, etc., of John and King Midas.

   Prepare a chart or Venn diagram to be used for comparing the stories of King Midas and John Midas. After reading *King Midas and the Golden Touch* and *The Chocolate Touch,* have the class brainstorm the similarities and differences in the plot or problem, setting, and characters for each selection. Write student ideas on the chart or Venn diagram. As an oral language extension, allow students to create stories based on a set of story components. (See the teacher's guide and Cooperative Story Creations activity on pages 44-46.) Then have students create a book report based on the imaginary situation described on pages 9-10.

4. John Midas' love for chocolate was no secret! Conduct a classroom survey to determine how much (or how little) students like chocolate. Distribute page 68 and have each student record his/her chocolate consumption for one week. Discuss results.

5. Students will have fun with poetry as they write odes and limericks about chocolate. Suggestions and samples are provided on pages 41-42.

Overview of Activities *(cont.)*

Enjoying the Book (cont.)

6. Prepare some of the food snacks on pages 69-70. Enjoy them in class while reading *The Chocolate Touch*. (Remind students that while there are beneficial nutrients in chocolate products, sweets are considered food choices to be consumed sparingly.)

7. Take a closer look at some of the ingredients that are used in chocolate candy. Have students read the labels from several brands of chocolate candies. Investigate the ingredients that are used in some candy-coated chocolate products with the science activity on page 51.

8. Have students practice their logic skills by solving the Chocolate Treats Logic Puzzle on page 47.

Extending The Book

1. Present this situation to the class: What if John Midas had not been cured? How would the town have changed? Brainstorm lists of changes that would occur in transportation, recreation, housing, and business. Do the problem-solving in the fishing industry activity on page 11. Allow students to present their creations to the class.

2. Have students imagine what it would be like to play a game, such as checkers, with John Midas. As he idly chews on a game piece, the entire game turns to chocolate! The Chocolate Checkers activity on pages 13-15 will give students an opportunity to simulate an experience that John and his friends might have encountered.

As students play Chocolate Checkers, they are introduced to ingredients that are often found in chocolate products. Have available resources about the origin and manufacture of chocolate. Once students are familiar with the game, introduce the probability activities on page 16.

3. Write imaginary book reports from the Chocolate City Library (pages 9-10). Allow students to share their reports.

Character Similarity

John Midas and King Midas had similar character traits, especially when it came to obsessions. Look up the word *obsession* in the dictionary. Think about ways in which John Midas and King Midas demonstrated an obsession. Fill in the obsession below for each character. Then answer the questions.

Obsession	John Midas	King Midas
most fond of:		
greedy for:		
all thoughts centered on:		
unconcerned about others because of:		

1. What happened when John got his wish of unlimited chocolate?

   _____

   _____

2. What happened when King Midas got his wish of unlimited gold?

   _____

   _____

3. What did John learn from *The Chocolate Touch* experience?

   _____

   _____

4. What lesson did King Midas learn in *The Golden Touch?*

   _____

   _____

5. A moral is a lesson learned through a story or event. What was the moral of both stories?

   _____

   _____

Check-Outs from the Chocolate Library

What types of books could boys and girls check-out from Chocolate City's library? What kinds of stories could be in the books? Would the stories have unusual settings? What characters would be in the stories?

Activity

Write a book report for an imaginary book from the Chocolate Library in Chocolate City. Brainstorm ideas for the title, author, setting, characters, and plot (the story line or problem to be solved). Write your ideas in the space below. After brainstorming, fill in the form on page 10.

Check-Out Form

Book Report

Title _____

Author _____

Setting   **Main Characters**

_____   _____

_____   _____

_____   _____

_____   _____

Plot

_____

_____

_____

_____

_____

_____

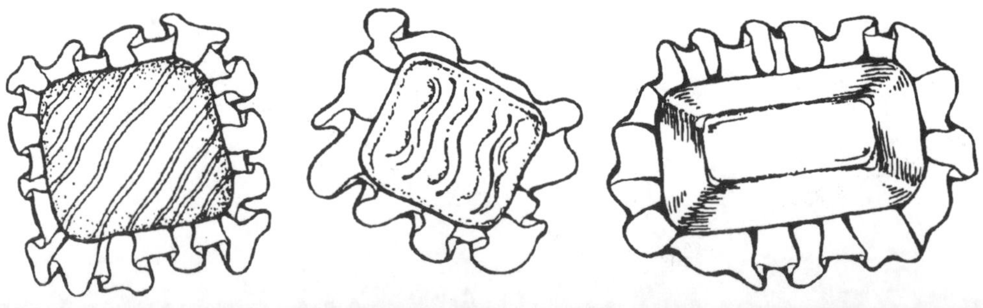

_____

The Fishing Industry in Chocolate City

The fishing industry needs help! Because of John Midas, everything has to be changed and updated. The fish are different. (Now there are fish with lips because the bait is so "lip-smacking" good.) The bait to be sold has to be changed. The fishing equipment must be improved. Rods, reels, fishing line, nets, hooks must be altered. Where and how the citizens fish must be regulated differently.

Activity

Complete the pamphlet below informing the citizens of Chocolate City of the changes in the fishing industry. Include a new set of fishing regulations to accommodate the changes.

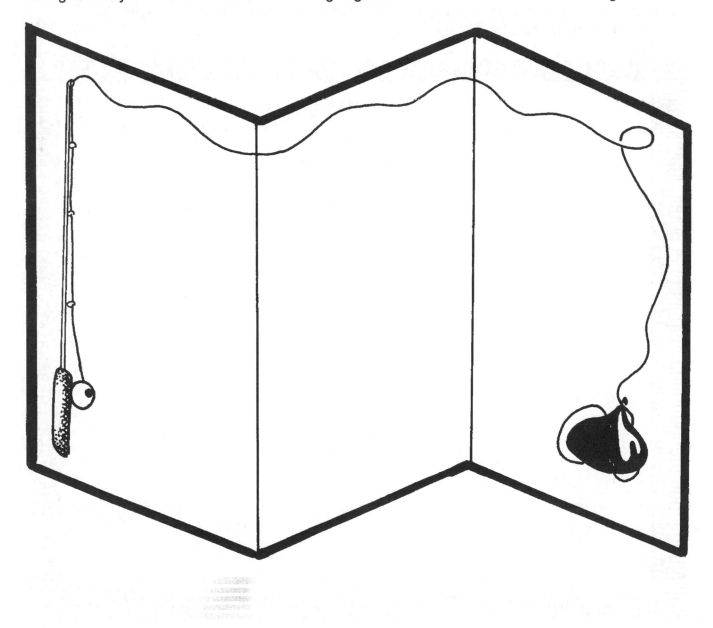

Problem Solving in Chocolate City's Clothing Industry

Thanks to John Midas, everything is now chocolate. There are problems to be solved in every city industry, and the garment industry is no exception. Imagine the dilemma clothing designers must face in creating clothing made of non-melting, smearless chocolate! Brainstorm some ideas that show what you would do in a situation like this. What problems might the designers encounter? Would the factory have to be specially designed and equipped?

Activity—"The Dress Mess"

One area of consideration in designing new clothing is the wording of garment labels. What special care directions do you think the clothing manufacturers should add to the labels? Write new instructions on the clothing label below.

Care Instructions

for_____

Chocolate Checkers

Teacher's Guide

The checkers game on pages 14-15 provides students with practice in problem solving using probability and the reinforcement of social skills.

The customary rules for checkers apply in Chocolate Checkers. Each player places 12 checkers on the black squares of the first 3 rows on opposite ends of the board. In order to capture all of the opponent's checkers, or block them so they cannot move, checkers are moved alternately forward in a diagonal direction. To capture an opponent's checker, the player must be able to jump (with his own checker) over the opponent's checker when there is a vacant square available. When a checker has reached the last row of the other player's side, it becomes a "king" which may move diagonally forward or backward. The "king" is identified by placing another checker on top of it. A player is allowed to jump as many of the other player's checkers on the same move as long as there are empty squares diagonally available after each checker. When a jump is available, the opponent must jump.

Materials: pages 14-15, reproduced (See preparation below.); probability practice activities on page 16 (See description below.); large manila envelopes (one per game board)

To Prepare the Game: For every two students, reproduce pages 14-15 on index paper. Cut out the board and checkers. If index paper is not available, reproduce the patterns on construction paper. Color checkers labeled "Brown" a light brown. Tape the two checker board pieces together to form a complete board. Laminate the board and checkers for durability. Store the board and checkers in a large manila folder or resealable plastic bag.

Playing the Game: In Chocolate Checkers, the checkers are placed ingredient-side up. Before the game begins, have each player set a goal indicating how many or which ingredient checkers they hope to capture. This allows opponents to plan strategies as they force each other into jumping ingredients not wanted or needed. It also allows strategic planning to obtain desired ingredients.

As a variation, place checkers ingredient-side down. This adds the element of surprise as students discover the ingredients obtained throughout the game.

Using Probability Practice: Pair students and provide each group with a set of checkers from the game and a large manila envelope. Distribute page 16 to each group. Guide students as they work in pairs to complete the page. Provide practice with probability using the following formula with activities such as flipping coins or drawing a specific color chip from a bag:

$$\textbf{Probability} = \frac{\text{Number of Favorable Outcomes}}{\text{Number of Possible Outcomes}}$$

Chocolate Checkers Game

White Checkers

CACAO BEANS

PALM OIL

CORN SYRUP

RAISINS

PEANUTS

BANANA CHIPS

ALMONDS

COCONUT

SUGAR

CACAO BEANS

COCONUT

MILK

Chocolate Checkers Game *(cont.)*

Brown Checkers

Chocolate Checkers Probability

Activity 1

In Chocolate Checkers, there are 24 ingredient checkers in the following amounts:

5 cacao bean	1 banana chip	1 palm oil	1 cashew
2 almond	3 sugar	2 corn syrup	1 milk
1 vanilla	2 peanut	2 coconut	1 oat
1 raisin	1 butter		

Place all 24 checkers in a large manila envelope. Use the following probability formula to answer the questions below. (You are allowed to draw one checker at a time.)

$$\text{Probability} = \frac{\text{Number of Favorable Outcomes}}{\text{Number of Possible Outcomes}}$$

1. If the ingredient you want is sugar, how many favorable outcomes are possible?_____

   What is the probability of drawing a sugar checker? _____

2. If you desire either sugar or corn syrup, how many favorable outcomes are possible? _____

   What is the probability of drawing either sugar or corn syrup? _____

3. If you wish to draw an almond checker, what is the probability that you will do so? _____

Activity 2

While playing Chocolate Checkers, the probability changes. The ingredients are divided in this way:

12 White Checkers		**12 Brown Checkers**	
2 coconut	2 cacao bean	3 cacao bean	1 cashew
1 almond	1 sugar	2 sugar	1 almond
1 peanut	1 corn syrup	1 peanut	1 butter
1 milk	1 banana chip	1 corn syrup	1 vanilla
1 raisin	1 palm oil	1 oat	

Use the information above to answer the following questions.
1. In a successful jump over a white checker, what is the probability of getting these ingredients?
   a. cacao beans _____
   b. raisins _____
   c. almonds, peanuts, or coconuts _____
2. In one jump over a brown checker, what is the probability of getting these ingredients?
   a. oats _____
   b. a sweetener_____
   c. some kind of nut _____

Charlie and the Chocolate Factory

by Roald Dahl

Summary

Charlie Bucket lives with his father, mother, and two sets of grandparents. They are very poor and have little to eat. However, a startling announcement by chocolate factory owner, Mr. Willy Wonka, changes all that. In his newspaper statement, Mr. Wonka announces that five lucky customers who find a "Golden Ticket" in one of his chocolate bars will be permitted to visit his factory for the first time to learn all his secrets and will each receive a lifetime supply of chocolates.

Charlie's "once a year" allotment for candy provides little hope for winning the contest. However, Charlie has the good fortune to find a dollar bill on the street, part of which he uses to buy Wonka bars. Miraculously, he finds the fifth "Golden Ticket!" Inside the factory, Charlie and the other four winners experience many exciting and unbelievable things. However, one by one children disappear because of their behaviors or actions, leaving Charlie to claim the greatest prize of all—inheritance of the entire Wonka factory.

The outline below is a suggested plan for using the various activities that are presented in this unit. You should adapt these to fit your own classroom situation.

Sample Plan

Lesson I

- Discuss the author and compare his books (page 18).
- Compare fictional and nonfictional story elements (page 18).
- Read chapters 1-12 of the selection.
- Classify fingerprints (pages 52-53).

Lesson II

- Read chapters 13-24.
- Complete Charlie's diary responses (page 25).
- Design golden tickets (page 27).
- Determine supply and demand for Mr. Wonka's chocolate (pages 22-24).
- Discover Spies in Mr. Wonka's Factory (pages 20-21).

Lesson III

- Read chapters 25-30 of the selection.
- Practice math skills using chocolate candy (pages 48-50).
- Determine the nutritional values of chocolate products (page 54).
- Create factory contraptions for new chocolate products (page 29).

Lesson IV

- Design candy wrappers (pages 64-66).
- Plan a room addition for Mr. Wonka's factory (page 28).
- Discover major chocolate consuming countries of the world (pages 57-58).
- Compare personality traits (page 26).

Overview of Activities

Setting the Stage
---

1. Roald Dahl is a well-known and popular author among young readers. Survey students to determine how many other Roald Dahl books they have read. (See Bibliography, page 80, for listing.) Compare some of these books, noting similarities and differences on a chart or chalk board. Encourage students to compare *Charlie and the Chocolate Factory* to Dahl's other books as they read the story. Stock a reading center with as many copies as possible of the author's books.

2. Ask students who have visited a candy factory to share their experiences with the class. Allow students to discuss what they imagine the inside of a chocolate factory to be like. Write their ideas on a large piece of paper. As students read *Charlie and the Chocolate Factory,* have them compare their ideas with the unique descriptions and functions of the rooms and machinery inside Mr. Wonka's factory.

3. Discuss the elements of a fictional and a nonfictional story. Ask students to provide examples of each. If possible, provide groups of students with a sampling of books related to the subject of candy. Have them analyze the books to determine whether they are fictional or nonfictional. As they read *Charlie and the Chocolate Factory,* encourage students to point out the fictional elements that comprise this adventure.

Enjoying the Book
---

1. Read chapters 1-12 of *Charlie and the Chocolate Factory.* Explain to students that a "Golden Ticket" is the key to adventure in *Charlie and the Chocolate Factory.* Distribute page 27 and ask students to write their own tickets for Mr. Wonka's contest. As an extension, have students design a ticket that would admit them to the adventure of a lifetime. What would the ticket look like? Ask students to describe the adventures they might experience.

2. Charlie faces some difficult decisions regarding the golden ticket. Ask students to read the situations presented on page 25. Have them record their responses, in diary form, and share their ideas with the class.

3. Grandpa Joe told Charlie the story of the secret workers and the jealous chocolate makers who sent spies to steal Mr. Wonka's recipes. Students will enjoy solving a mystery as they test the ink on a mystery note. A teacher's guide and student enrichment activity are provided on pages 20-21.

4. Ask students if they think Mr. Wonka could have captured the spies more easily through fingerprint identification of his factory workers. Discuss with students the technique of fingerprinting as a method of identification. (Many students may have fingerprints on file through school-sponsored projects or public service organizations.) Allow students to practice fingerprinting with the student activity on page 53. A teacher's guide for fingerprint classification is found on page 52.

Overview of Activities *(cont.)*

Enjoying the Book (cont.)

---

5. Discuss the terms "supply" and "demand" and what they might mean to the success of a business such as Mr. Wonka's. Simulate a supply and demand situation in the classroom by providing a limited number of a "valued" item to a group and creating a great demand for the item. (Reverse the process, with an oversupply of an item and decreased demand for it.) Discuss what happens to the price of the item in each situation. Have students complete the supply/demand activities on pages 22-24.

6. Ask students to compare and contrast the personality traits of Charlie, Violet, Mike, Augustus, and Veruca. After completing the information in the candy box on page 26, have students share their responses with the class.

7. Provide students with practice in math skills and recording/graphing data as they complete the manipulative activities on pages 49-50. A teacher's guide is provided on page 48.

Extending the Book

---

1. Reproduce and distribute page 28 to students. Encourage students to use their imaginations to create a room addition for Mr. Wonka's factory. Have them share their designs with the class. As an extension, students can design a Rube Goldberg style candy machine for their room addition. Information and suggestions are provided on page 29.

2. Ask students to bring in chocolate candy wrappers. Divide the class into small groups and distribute some wrappers to each group. Discuss the ingredients labelling on the wrappers. Note the most commonly listed nutrients and discuss the health benefit of each. Use the information and questions on page 54 to determine the nutritional values listed on five of the wrappers. Discuss the results of the investigation.

3. Take a class poll to determine how many pounds (kg) of chocolate students think they consume in one year. Ask students which countries they feel consume the most chocolate. List their responses. Direct students to use the information on page 57 to complete the pictograph on page 58 representing the chocolate consumption of several countries.

4. Have students design candy wrappers. Collect candy wrappers for students to view. Observe the designs, names, colors, ingredient labels, etc. Allow students to create their own wrappers using the information and patterns on pages 64-66. Display the finished products around the room.

Spies in the Wonka Factory
Teacher's Guide

Use the information and enrichment activity on this page to help students solve the mystery on page 21.

Materials

- solvent (water, alcohol, white vinegar, ammonia)
- several different brand black felt-tip markers
- filter paper (coffee filters work well)
- toothpicks
- clean containers (narrow glasses or jars)
- scissors
- copies of page 21, reproduced for each group of 2-3 students

Preparation

- Prepare a note (or notes depending on the number of groups in the class) with black marker. Notes written on coffee filters seem to work best.

- **NOTE:** Permanent markers are not water soluble and will not display colors.

- Cut coffee filters into strips. The lengths should be as long as the jars are tall to provide ample length for the strip to touch the solvent.

- Place students in groups of 2-3.

- This activity is actually a demonstration of paper chromatography, a procedure frequently used in laboratories to separate mixtures into their individual components.

- Students will be amazed at the number of colors in "black" markers.

Enrichment

- Use different solvents such as rubbing alcohol, white vinegar, and ammonia. Have students decide which solvent works best (gives the widest color separation) for each marker.

- On a chart similar to the one below, have students record the colors they observed in the appropriate boxes.

Marker (number/type)	Solvent			
	water	rubbing alcohol	white vinegar	ammonia
#1				
#2				
#3				

20

Spies in the Wonka Factory

Mr. Willy Wonka needs help finding the workers who are stealing his recipes. He has some items with fingerprints and a note which was found near the items. One Oompa-Loompa suggested testing the ink on the note. If it could be determined what type of black pen was used, then this clue might lead to a suspect.

Follow the steps to learn how to test the black markers. When you have recorded your observations, the teacher will give your group a part of the note to test. Decide which marker was used.

Materials: 2 or 3 different types of black felt-tip markers; narrow glass or jar; filter paper cut in strips about the length of the glass jar; toothpicks; solvent (water)

Directions

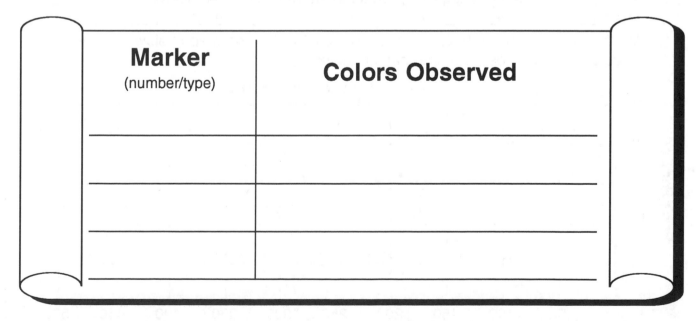

1. Pour 2 tablespoons (30 mL) of solvent (water) into the glass container or jar.
2. Use a pencil to label the top of each filter strip so you will know which marker is being tested. (You will need the same number of filter strips and toothpicks as there are markers to test.)
3. Push a toothpick through the top end of the filter paper.
4. Use one of the markers to make a dot in the middle of the filter paper.
5. Rest the toothpick on the jar rim so that the filter paper is suspended from the toothpick and touches the solvent.
6. Repeat the process using the remaining markers.
7. Record your observations of the reactions and color separations below.

Marker (number/type)	Colors Observed

After you have collected the data concerning the black markers, you are ready to test the ink on the "mystery note" supplied by your teacher.

Demand for Wonka Chocolate

CONSUMERS are purchasers of goods and services. Once a year for his birthday, Charlie Bucket was a consumer of Wonka Chocolate.

Mr. Wonka continued throughout the year to SUPPLY the amount of candy. CONSUMERS would buy based on the DEMAND for the goods.

Below are the results of a market survey which determines the DEMAND for the Wonka Bar. The survey shows how many chocolate bars consumers would buy at different prices.

Demand Chart

Price (per bar)	Number of Bars Consumers Would Buy	Revenue from Sales
.50	50	$25.00
.40	150	_____
.30	250	_____
.20	350	_____
.10	450	_____

Activities

1. The example in the third column (Revenue from Sales) indicates that consumers would buy 50 bars at a price of $.50 per bar, creating a revenue (income) of $25.00 ($.50 x 50 = $25.00). Fill in the remainder of the chart.

2. If Willy Wonka wants to sell the most chocolate bars, which price should he charge? _____

3. Which price should he charge if he wants to earn the most revenues? _____
   Why?_____

4. Use the information you have gathered to complete the line graph below. Connect the points to show the results of the market survey.

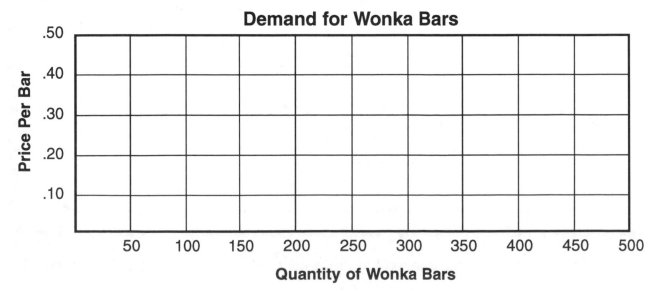

Demand for Wonka Bars

Supplying Wonka Bars

Mr. Wonka must figure out how many Wonka Bars to produce. The market survey revealed how many chocolate bars consumers would buy at different prices (demand), but now Mr. Wonka needs to consider the quantity and price of his chocolate bars. Help Mr. Wonka analyze the SUPPLY side of his business by using the chart and activities below to complete the supply graph at the bottom of the page.

Supply Chart

Price (per bar)	Quantity of Bars Mr. Wonka Would Supply
.50	500
.40	400
.30	250
.20	150
.10	50

Activities

1. At what price can Mr. Wonka supply the most chocolate bars? _____
2. At what price can he supply the fewest chocolate bars? _____
3. As the candy price goes up, what happens to the quantity supplied? _____
4. As the candy price goes down, what happens to the quantity supplied? _____
5. Use the information you have gathered to complete the line graph below to show the supply schedule for Mr. Wonka's chocolate bar production.

Supply Graph for Wonka Chocolate Bars

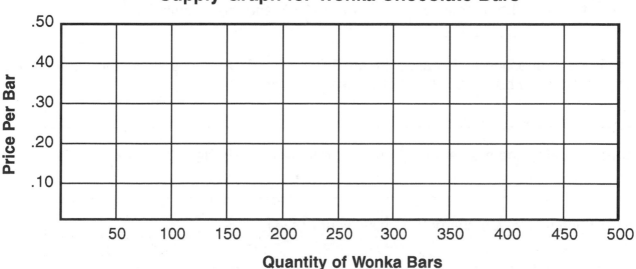

How Many Wonka Bars?

Supply and Demand

Mr. Willy Wonka is now ready to decide how many chocolate bars to produce and what price to charge for each bar. Use the "Demand Chart" and "Supply Chart" information from pages 22 and 23 to plot the demand and supply schedules on the graph below. (Use a different color to represent each line. Write the colors in the key.) Then, answer the questions at the bottom of the page. Be prepared to discuss with classmates what you discovered about supply and demand.

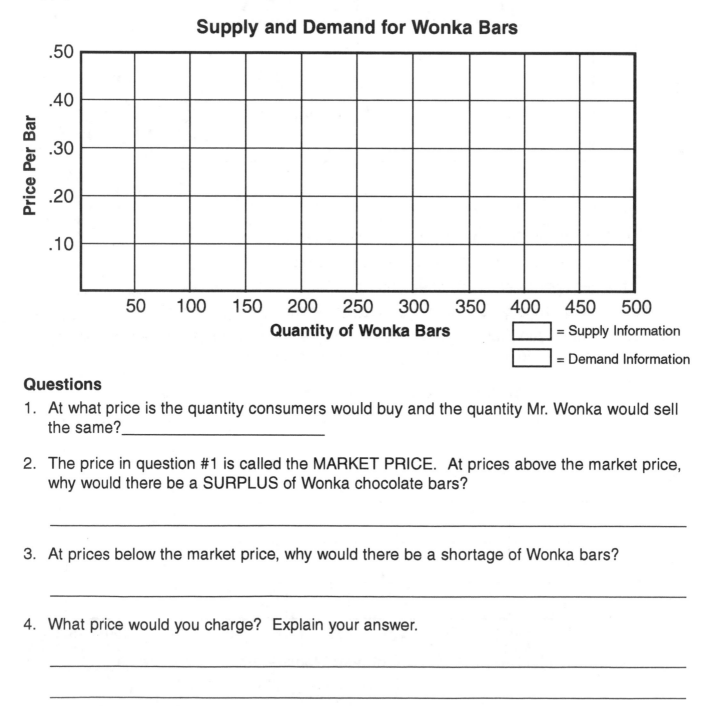

Questions

1. At what price is the quantity consumers would buy and the quantity Mr. Wonka would sell the same?_____

2. The price in question #1 is called the MARKET PRICE. At prices above the market price, why would there be a SURPLUS of Wonka chocolate bars?

   _____

3. At prices below the market price, why would there be a shortage of Wonka bars?

   _____

4. What price would you charge? Explain your answer.

   _____

   _____

Decisions, Decisions!

Charlie is faced with many difficult decisions both in and out of the chocolate factory. Most choices were based on his own conscience about what to do in each situation.

Put yourself in Charlie's place as you read the situations below. Try to imagine what Charlie would write in a diary as he responds to each decision-making situation described below. Write Charlie's diary entries in the space provided.

Situation	Charlie's Response
Grandpa Joe gives Charlie a dime to get a Wonka chocolate bar. Grandpa Joe is hoping they might find the golden ticket. Grandpa Joe asks Charlie not to tell anyone in the family about their scheme. Charlie has to decide whether he should keep this to himself or ask his parents if he should spend the money on candy.	Dear Diary,
Charlie feels very lucky when he finds a one dollar bill. Charlie knows that his family is at the point of starvation, especially now that his father has lost his job at the toothpaste factory. Charlie has to decide whether he should give this money to his parents or spend it on candy.	Dear Diary,
Once Charlie finds the golden ticket, he is offered large sums of money from people. A woman offers him five hundred dollars. Charlie's family is in desperate need of money. Charlie has to decide whether he should keep the golden ticket or sell it so his family will have money for food.	Dear Diary,

You've Got Personality!

Each of the five children in *Charlie and the Chocolate Factory* has a distinct personality. Yet, in some ways they are very much alike. In the candy box below, list as many personality traits as you can for each character. On the back of this paper, list the ways in which the characters are alike and the ways in which they are different. Decide which one is your favorite and explain why.

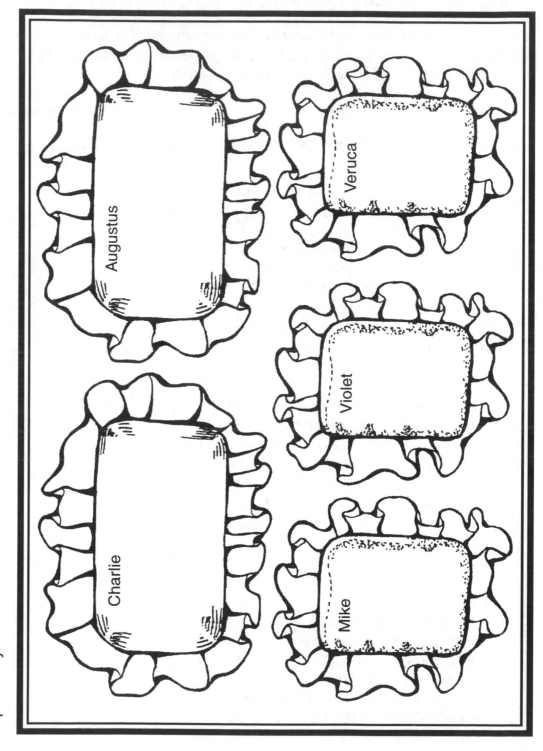

Write Your Own Ticket

A statement made by Willy regarding his contest and the golden tickets appeared in the *Evening Bulletin*. As you can imagine, the news created quite a stir among young and old alike as they searched for one of the five golden tickets hidden inside Mr. Wonka's chocolate bars.

Imagine that you have been offered the chance to design the famous golden ticket. In the box below, create your own design for a golden ticket. Then, use your own words to tell others about the particulars of the contest. Share your ticket and statements with the class.

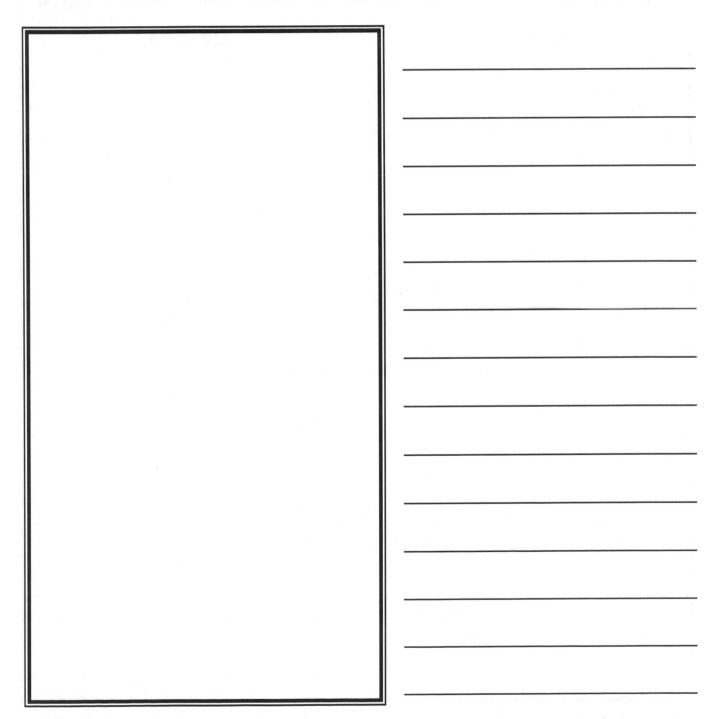

A Factory Addition

You were introduced to some unusual candy-making devices and rooms in Mr. Wonka's chocolate factory. Roald Dahl provided vivid descriptions of these rooms. For this activity, you will create and illustrate a new room for the candy factory. In this room, a new kind of candy will be manufactured. Use the space below for your illustration. Include as many details and labels as possible. Present your illustration to the class and explain how the machinery in it works.

THE _____ ROOM

Creative Contraptions

When it comes to contraptions, Rube Goldberg was one of the best designers of all. He was a newspaper cartoonist who drew very complicated contraptions that performed very simple tasks. Although these designs were impractical for everyday tasks, his cartoon inventions showed a complicated sequence of tasks that somehow, incredibly got the job done. A Rube Goldberg contraption has a series of actions, each one causing the next action to begin.

The Oompa-Loompas have constructed a Rube Goldberg contraption which will give them a five-minute break in the factory. At the end of their Rube Goldberg device, there is a bucket set to hurl melted chocolate into the air. As the chocolate falls, it splatters into the mixture, creating Splatter Bars.

Activity

What type of strange, new candy are candy-lovers of the world eagerly awaiting? Perhaps a chocolate pencil is needed to use in school so you can snack while writing, or a new candy can be created that cleans your teeth.

Create a candy-making machine that will make a chocolate product that boys and girls everywhere will want. Use the space below to design the machine that makes the new candy.

Vanilla, Chocolate, & Strawberry

by Bonnie Busenberg

Summary

Chocolate is probably the world's most favorite food, but where did it come from and how did it become so popular? The middle section of the book *Vanilla, Chocolate, & Strawberry* traces the advent of chocolate into North America from its early beginnings in Mexico. It chronicles how ancient explorers brought chocolate back to Spain where it was kept a closely guarded secret and how, through the years, it eventually was introduced to other countries. In addition to the history of the flavor, the book tells all about the growing and processing of cacao, the different types of chocolate, contributions made by different choclatiers, and even some medicinal and nutritional values of chocolate.

The remaining sections of the selection explore two other popular flavors — vanilla and strawberry — in much the same way as the chocolate section. Diagrams, pictures, and sumptuous photographs throughout make this a very appealing book and perfect support reading for a chocolate unit.

The outline below is a suggested plan for using the various activities that are presented in this unit. You should adapt these ideas to fit your own classroom situation.

Sample Plan

Lesson I

- Display forms of chocolate and sample chocolate (page 31).
- Begin reading about chocolate in *Vanilla, Chocolate, & Strawberry*.
- Choose and complete one or more "Critical Thinking" Text Enhancers (page 33).
- Explore "chocolate" words (page 36).

Lesson II

- Make a flow chart of the curing process (page 33).
- Review the legend of Quetzalcoatl and write a modern version (page 33).
- Choose and complete one or more "Social Studies" Text Enhancers (pages 33-34).
- Create a chocolate collage (page 32).

Lesson III

- Use information from the selection to solve math problems (page 40).
- Choose and complete one or more "Science" Text Enhancers (page 34).
- Experience chocolate through writing (page 37).

- Finish reading *Vanilla, Chocolate, & Strawberry*. Compare information about each flavor (page 32).
- Make a class mural (page 32).

Lesson IV

- Choose and complete one or more "Math" Text Enhancers (page 35).
- Learn about famous names in chocolate (page 39).
- Create pod pictures using "Art" Text Enhancers (page 35).
- Assign ingredients activity from "Homework" Text Enhancers (page 35).
- Discover the countries that export chocolate ingredients (pages 59-61).

Lesson V

- Choose and complete one or more "Whole Book Extensions" from Text Enhancers (page 35).
- Assign cocoa butter activity from "Homework" Text Enhancers (page 35).
- Make Trivia Wheels (pages 62-63).
- Complete a puzzle about chocolate (page 38).

Overview of Activities

Setting the Stage

---

1. If there is a chocolate factory in your area plan a class visit to the facility. As an alternative, write to a chocolate factory, such as Hershey®, Mars®, Brach®, or Nestlé® for some brochures and information about their facilities. (See page 80 for addresses.)

2. Prepare a display of the different types of chocolate in its many forms: semi-sweet baking chocolate, chocolate chips, cocoa, chocolate bars, etc. Have a tasting party where the students can sample each. Discuss which forms of chocolate they like best.

3. Have on hand a number of chocolate cookbooks. Check your local bookstore and library for these specialty cookbooks. Direct the students to look through them and choose a recipe they might like to try.

4. Tell students that the first chocolate bars were made in the 1840s by John and Benjamin Cadbury and Joseph Fry. Cadbury's chocolate can still be found in markets today. Bring in various brands of chocolate bars for the students to sample.

5. Read aloud (or assign students to read) the pages about chocolate from the book *Vanilla, Chocolate, & Strawberry*.

Enjoying the Book

---

1. Reinforce the text with any or all of the activities presented on the three Text Enhancers pages (pages 33-35). They encompass math, science, social studies, art, critical thinking, creative writing, and life skills. Assign different projects to each group of students or choose one activity for the whole class to work on. Use as many of the projects as you need to reinforce and extend the text.

2. Expand the students' vocabulary with activities and projects presented on page 36. Assign groups of students to complete different activities or allow students a choice of assignments from the page. Suggested words have already been chosen, but you may want to supply your own from the text. With the whole class, brainstorm some chocolate-related words. Enlarge the pattern on page 77. List the words in the pattern. Add new words to the list throughout the unit.

3. Have some fun with the creative writing projects on page 37. Students will especially enjoy writing chocolate poetry. With this assignment it's best to have extra chocolate treats on hand for those who just can't wait. Other creative writing ideas on this page include designing ads for chocolate, creating chocolate tongue twisters, and writing chocolate slogans.

4. What better way to review what they have learned about chocolate than a crossword puzzle! All the answers to the puzzle on page 38 are related to the making of chocolate.

Overview of Activities

5. Students can review some of the famous names in chocolate with the activity on page 39. If preferred, this page can be presented as a group, oral exercise. List the names of the chocolate contributors on the chalkboard for all to see. Read a description aloud. Call on a student to come to the board and circle the correct answer. Repeat until all names have been identified.

6. All the math problems on page 40 are directly related to the text of *Vanilla, Chocolate, & Strawberry*. The problems can be solved individually or in student pairs. Problems may also be presented orally for students to solve the problems at their seats. Have volunteers explain how they arrived at their answers and tell what operations they used to solve the problems.

7. Use the teacher's guide provided on page 59 to prepare students for the activities on pages 60-61. **Note:** have extra copies of page 60 on hand for students to record information.

Extending the Book

1. Read the remaining two sections of the *Vanilla, Chocolate, & Strawberry* book. Compare those two sections with the text about chocolate. How does their production differ? How are the flavors prepared? Are they used only in cooking or in other areas? Make a class chart comparing and contrasting the three flavors. Taste samples of the three flavors. Vote on the class favorite. Make a pie graph or bar graph based on the results of the voting.

2. Make a class mural showing how chocolate is made. Assign some text to each group of students and have them design illustrations for that section of text. Display the pages in chronological order on a classroom wall.

3. Sample chocolate in as many forms as possible—bars, syrup, cocoa, etc. Visit a grocery store to find chocolate in these forms. Is there any other area in which chocolate could be used but isn't? Have the students invent a new use for chocolate.

4. Create a collage using pieces of chocolate (small shapes work best) and candy wrappers. Cut out chocolate ads from magazines. Arrange the objects on a sheet of tagboard or other heavy paper. When the arrangement is complete, glue the pieces to the tagboard. Shellac the whole surface to preserve the piece. Be sure to do this step in a well-ventilated room, or better yet, outdoors.

5. Prepare the wheel as directed on pages 62-63. Students can complete the statements by matching the information on the top and bottom wheels. **Option:** Prepare a blank Trivia Wheel on which you write your own chocolate trivia statements. Simply use correction tape to delete the wheel information on both wheels before reproducing the pages.

Text Enhancers

The activities below and on pages 34 and 35 can be used to extend the reading of the text. These projects encompass all areas of the curriculum from reading to science to art. Choose those which best fit your classroom needs and your teaching style.

Critical Thinking

- Chocolate is the secret ingredient in many substances. Review the different ways it is used. *(Knowledge)*

- After reading the section about curing cacao beans, assign students to groups. Instruct them to make a flow chart showing the step-by-step processes involved. Pictures may be drawn to illustrate each step. Have each group explain its chart to the rest of the class. *(Knowledge)*

- Make a chart showing the differences between milk chocolate, semisweet chocolate, and sweet chocolate. Include statistics about government specifications for each. *(Analysis)*

- Examine the differences between brown chocolate and white chocolate. *(Comprehension)*

- Discuss why chocolate is so difficult to duplicate chemically. *(Comprehension)*

Creative Writing

- Read the legend of Quetzalcoatl; reread it, if necessary. Pair the students and have them write a modern version of this tale. Tell them they are inhabitants of a new planet and have never heard of chocolate until one day a new being appears with news of this unheard-of drink. Have students illustrate the stories. Share stories in class.

- In one or two paragraphs have students defend this statement: *Chocolate is good for you.* (For additional creative writing projects see page 37.)

Social Studies

- Hernan Cortés (Hernando Cortez) was not the god that the Aztecs had hoped for. Instead, he imprisoned their king and savagely destroyed their country. Learn more about Cortés and the Aztecs. Many fine activities can be found in Teacher Created Materials' thematic book #288 - *Explorers*. Students can also read encyclopedias, history texts, and support books such as *Cortés and the Conquest of Mexico* by Bernard Diaz del Castillo (Linnet Books, 1988).

- Encourage students to research the growth of the cacao tree and the spread in popularity of chocolate throughout the world. Have students work individually or in groups to complete the activity and map on pages 55-56. As an extension, make a time line showing how chocolate was distributed from Mexico to Spain to other countries of the world. Write and illustrate each event on a separate large index card. Tape the cards in chronological order on a classroom wall or door.

Text Enhancers *(cont.)*

Social Studies *(cont.)*

• Arrange students in pairs or small groups. Direct them to draw a world map (or use the map on page 56). Have them locate and label the areas where cacao plantations have been established. Next to each area, write the name of the country that controls those plantations. (See pages 50-51 in *Vanilla, Chocolate, & Strawberry* for a complete listing of nations.)

• Review the accomplishments of the names presented on pages 62 and 63 of *Vanilla, Chocolate, & Strawberry*. Students can complete the activity Who's Who in Chocolate on page 39. If preferred, present it as an oral activity. On the chalkboard, write the names from the Name Box for all to view. Read the descriptions one at a time. Call on a student to come to the board and circle the correct name. Repeat until all descriptions have been read.

Science

• *Theobroma cacao* is the scientific name of the cacao tree. Learn some other scientific names for common trees in your area. Make a list of some of the native trees of your region. Assign students the task of finding out and write the scientific name of each tree listed.

• Tell students to draw, color, and label the parts of a cacao tree. On the same paper have them draw a cross section of a cacao pod. Label and color the diagram.

• Describe the conditions in which cacao grows best. Reread the text if necessary.

• Chocolate contains many compounds including caffeine and theobromine. Have the students make 3-D models of these compounds.

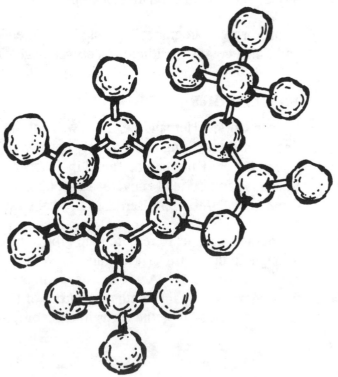

Materials: red, purple, blue, and green modeling clay or gumdrops; toothpicks; a copy of the compounds on page 68 of *Vanilla, Chocolate, & Strawberry*.

Directions: Roll the clay into pea-sized balls. (Refer to the diagram on page 68 of the book so you know how many of each color to make.)

Connect the colored balls or gumdrops with toothpicks. (Refer to the diagram for help.)

Extension: Examine and compare both models. How are the two compounds alike? What is the main difference between them? What effect does each compound have in the human body?

Text Enhancers *(cont.)*

Math

- Ancient natives of Mexico valued chocolate so much that they used cacao beans as a type of money. Among the Mayas, for example, 8 beans could buy a rabbit but it would take 100 beans to purchase a slave. Divide the students into small groups. Instruct them to write a list of some of their favorite chocolate treats—ice cream bars, candy bars, kisses, etc. Draw a picture of each one or attach a wrapper from that treat to a large sheet of tagboard to make a chart. Next to each chocolate item write the number of cacao beans that they think each is worth. The whole group must decide and agree on the value of each item. Display all the completed charts.

- Provide students with a taste of vanilla, chocolate, and strawberry in any form you choose. Have them rank the three flavors in order of their preference from the most-liked to the least-liked. Create a class chart of the resulting data. (Additional math problems can be found on page 40.)

Art

- Cacao trees are very colorful because the pods may be red, yellow, gold, pale green, or a mixture of these colors. Have the students create their own pod pictures.

  Materials: Colored art tissue; scissors; white glue; water; plastic margarine cups; paintbrushes; tagboard or other heavy paper

  Directions: In the cup, add water to glue to thin it; set the mixture aside. Cut the art tissue into pod shapes. Make at least three cut-outs for each pod. Glue the tissue to the tagboard. Cover the pod with another layer of tissue and glue. Add a third layer in the same manner.

  Repeat this process for all the pods. Overlap the shapes to produce colorful results.

Homework

- As a homework assignment, tell the students to check the ingredients on bread wrappers, cereal boxes, and other foods in their kitchen pantries. Discuss the findings next day in class.

- Cocoa butter can be found in many cosmetics, sun tan lotions, and soaps. Have the students check at home or in stores for any products that contain cocoa butter. Make a list of these products on chart paper.

Whole Book Extensions

- Read the text about vanilla and strawberry. Make a chart comparing the three flavors. Include areas such as the molecular structure of compounds in each flavor, ways each flavor is used, how each flavor is extracted and prepared, the origin of each flavor, its history, areas where it is grown, and pictures of the plants that produce each flavor.

- Read *Chocolate Fever* by Robert Kimmel Smith (Dell Publishing, 1972). Tell the students to write some adventures using one of these titles: "Vanilla Fever"; "Strawberry Fever"; "The Vanilla-Strawberry Fields".

- Conduct a contest for the best recipe for a vanilla, chocolate, and strawberry dessert! Get another teacher or a parent volunteer to do the judging.

Chocolate Words

Any number of words can be extracted from the text for use in developing and expanding vocabulary. Some suggested vocabulary words appear below along with a number of related activities.

Vocabulary

chocoholic	ferment	tempering	phenylethylamine
Quetzalcoatl	enzymes	cacao emulsifier	chocolate liqueur
caffeine	nibs	lecithin	flavor precursors
chocolatl	theobromine	distilling	choclatiers
molinet	cocoa butter	volatile	
theobroma	refining	amino acids	
plantations	conching	roast	

Activities

• **Research**—On a large sheet of tagboard or butcher paper draw an outline of a chocolate kiss (enlarge the pattern from page 77, if desired). Cut out the shape and attach it to a wall or bulletin board. Write a list of vocabulary words on the surface of the shape, leaving room for more words. As the students read other references and learn more about chocolate have them add appropriate words to the list.

• **Chocolate Connections**—Write the vocabulary words on the chalkboard or overhead projector for all to see. Assign pairs of students to copy each word and tell how each is connected to chocolate. In a large group, review their definitions.

• **Categories**—Classify the words into different categories. Write a category name on the chalkboard (e.g., Chemical Names, Processing Terms, or Different Forms of Chocolate.) Call on students to come to the board and write a word that fits in that category. **Variation:** Tell the students to choose their own category and write all the vocabulary words that belong in that group.

• **Morphing**—One base word can be changed into many forms. From chocolate we get chocoholic, chocolatl, and choclatiers. Using their knowledge of prefixes and suffixes, have the students invent some new chocolate-based words and write a definition for each. The word choclatess, for example, might mean a female who likes chocolate. Have students write the words on separate index cards. Alphabetize them and store in an index card file box.

• **Chocolate Sentences**—Display the vocabulary word list on the chalkboard or overhead projector for all to view. Make sure the students have paper and pencil on hand. Call out any three words and have the students write a sentence using all three words. Ask for volunteers to share their sentences with the rest of the class. Continue in the same manner until at least five sentences have been written.

A Creative Touch

Presented on this page are a number of creative writing topics with one common theme — chocolate. Assign any number of them to large or small groups. Or, make a copy of this page for each student; require them to choose and complete a specified number of projects on the page.

- **Chocoholic**—Read *Chocolate Fever* by Robert Kimmel Smith (Dell Publishing, 1972) to find out what a true chocoholic's life might be like. Write some of your own adventures as a chocoholic. Use any of these titles: "Chocoholic's Worst Nightmare", "The Day I Became a Chocoholic", and "The Facts About Chocoholics".

- **Chocolate Poetry**—Give each student one foil-wrapped chocolate candy and a number of index cards or strips of construction paper. Instruct them to remove the foil but do not eat the candy at this time! First, have them observe the chocolate candy and describe its color, shape, texture, etc. Tell them to write one descriptive word per card or strip, using as many as they want. Next, have them smell the chocolate candy; write descriptive words. Finally, taste the chocolate and write some more descriptive words. As the students are eating, have them arrange their words into a poem. Share the word poems with the rest of the class. Afterwards, share some chocolate poetry with the class. An interesting assortment can be found in *Chocolate Dreams* by Arnold Adoff (Lothrop, Lee & Shepard Books, 1989) and *The Chocolate Book* selected by Michael Patrick Hearn (Caedmon, 1983).

- **Tongue Twisters**—Read aloud some of the chocolate tongue twisters found in *The Chocolate Book* selected by Michael Patrick Hearn (Caedmon, 1983). After the class has had fun practicing them, ask the students to write their own chocolate tongue twisters.

- **History**—Learn the history of Toll House® cookies and how chocolate chips were invented. A good resource for this information is *Steven Caney's Invention Book* by Steven Caney (Workman Publishing, 1985). Have the students write a history of some other form of chocolate such as peanut butter cups, M & M's®, or chocolate covered raisins.

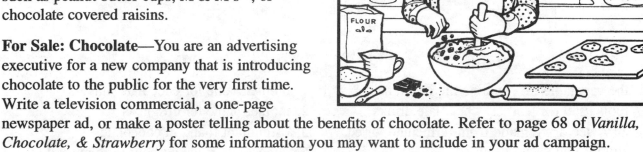

- **For Sale: Chocolate**—You are an advertising executive for a new company that is introducing chocolate to the public for the very first time. Write a television commercial, a one-page newspaper ad, or make a poster telling about the benefits of chocolate. Refer to page 68 of *Vanilla, Chocolate, & Strawberry* for some information you may want to include in your ad campaign.

- **Slogans**—Most students have been exposed to television, radio, or magazine slogans about chocolate or other sweets. Have the class brainstorm a list of chocolate candies and some of the slogans that are associated with them. Tell them to choose five forms of chocolate candies and write an appropriate slogan for each. Ask students to share the slogans with the class.

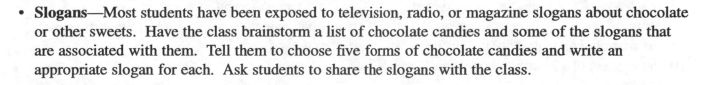

Vanilla, Chocolate, & Strawberry

Chocolate Crossword Puzzle

All of the words in the crossword puzzle below are related in some way to chocolate and the making of chocolate. Read each clue and write the correct answer in the corresponding spaces of the puzzle. Some clues have been given to help you get started.

Across

1. the vegetable fat contained in cacao beans
3. tools used for frothing chocolate drinks
4. an Aztec drink made from fermented, dried, and ground cacao beans
7. roasted cacao beans with the seed coats removed
8. the first chocolate makers in Europe
10. the process of kneading chocolate after it has been refined
11. the process of gradually cooling chocolate

Down

1. another name for chocolate makers
2. another name for druggists
5. a stimulant found in chocolate
6. a chocolate made without milk but with a moderate amount of sugar
9. fine, chocolate powder used in making cakes and candy

Who's Who in Chocolate

Over the years a number of people have contributed to the distribution, processing, and production of chocolate in all of its many forms. See how many of these people you can identify. Read each description below. Write the name of the contributor on the line at the beginning of the sentence. Use the name box at the bottom of the page if necessary.

1. _____ This Irish chocolate maker was the first to import cacao beans to the American colonies directly from the Caribbean islands.

2. _____ He developed a process called conching in which chocolate is kneaded. The process is named after the shell-shaped troughs originally used during kneading.

3. _____ Not only did he start a chocolate factory in Pennsylvania, but he also built a whole town complete with houses, businesses, restaurants, and schools.

4. _____ In 1810, this chemist developed the process for making cocoa. He also invented another type of cocoa named "Dutch" because he was from Holland.

5. _____ When he arrived in Mexico in 1519, he discovered chocolate, a favorite national drink in that country. Nine years later he returned to Spain with that country's first cacao beans.

6. _____ This Aztec king treated the explorer, Cortés, like royalty. Great feasts were concluded with the serving of chocolatl, a favorite drink, in golden cups.

7. _____ A doctor from Massachusetts, he was partners with John Hannon. He was a financial backer in the import of cacao beans because he knew that chocolate was in great demand by apothecaries.

8. _____ In addition to inventing condensed milk, this French Swiss contributed to the creation of milk chocolate. His name is still famous in the chocolate industry.

9. _____ He is another Swiss who is famous in the chocolate industry. He started manufacturing chocolate in his home land in 1899.

10. _____ These English brothers, John and Benjamin, were staunch Quakers. Along with Joseph Fry they made the first chocolate bars in the 1840s.

Name Box

Henri Nestlé	Randolphe Lindt
Coenraad van Houten	Jean Tobler
Hernan Cortés	James Baker
Cadbury	Montezuma II
John Hannon	Milton Hershey

Textbook Math

The facts and figures for all of the problems below come straight from the text of *Vanilla, Chocolate, & Strawberry*. Use the information given to solve the problems. Write your answer on the line after the problem.

1. Americans eat almost 11 pounds (5kg) of chocolate per person per year. That is only half the amount of chocolate consumed by Europeans annually.

   a. How many pounds (kg) of chocolate per person per year do Europeans consume? _____

   b. If the population of the United States is 250,000,000, how many pounds (kg) of chocolate are consumed in one year? _____

2. It is said that Montezuma drank more than 50 cups (11.3L) of chocolate per day and that his household consumed more than 2,000 cups (452L) of chocolate per day.

   a. How many cups (L) of chocolate did Montezuma personally drink per week? _____

   b. How many cups (L) did he drink in a 31-day month? _____

   c. How many cups (L) of chocolate did Montezuma's household consume per week? _____

3. Each cacao tree produces 20 to 50 pods per year, enough to make 5 to 13 pounds (2 kg-6 kg) of processed chocolate. Each pod weighs about one pound (.45 kg).

   a. If a plantation owner has 150 cacao trees what is the least number of pounds (kg) of processed chocolate he/she will make? _____

   b. If a plantation owner has 205 cacao trees what is the greatest number of pounds (kg) the pods will weigh? _____

4. A 3.5-ounce (98g) chocolate bar contains about 500 calories. About how many calories are there in 4, 3.5-ounce (98g) chocolate bars? _____

5. In their natural state, cacao trees grow as tall as 50 feet. On plantations, however, trees are kept at about 25 feet to make harvesting easier.

   a. How many meters tall can cacao trees grow in their natural state?

   _____

   b. About how many yards tall are trees on plantations allowed to grow?

   _____

Ode to Chocolate

An *ode* is a type of poem written in honor of something or someone. It is made of more than one stanza. Each stanza has four lines which can rhyme in different ways. The last words of the first and third lines can rhyme or the last words of the second and fourth lines can rhyme. An ode may even rhyme, both ways.

Example:

> *Cocoa is brown,*
> *Chocolate is sweet,*
> *Buying candy in town,*
> *Is the very best treat.*
> *Sugar is added,*
> *Milk is too,*
> *Making chocolate sweet and creamy,*
> *For me and for you.*
> *If I could switch,*
> *To a better treat,*
> *It would be to one,*
> *That's not messy, but neat.*

Use your feelings about and experiences with chocolate to write your own ode to chocolate. On the lines below, list rhyming words that you might use in your poem. Think of words that describe something about chocolate, how it tastes, what comes to mind when you think of chocolate, etc. On a separate piece of paper, write an ode to chocolate using your list of ideas. Add a decorative border.

Lickable Limericks

A *limerick* is a short, foolish poem. The key element in a limerick is humor. Most limericks are five lines long and follow these rules:

Lines 1, 2, 5 rhyme and have 8-10 syllables.

Lines 3, 4, rhyme and have 5-7 syllables.

Here is an example of a limerick.

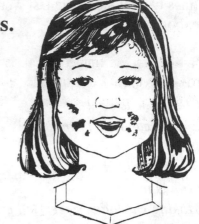

There once was a woman named Grace,
Who wore chocolate all over her face.
When asked why that's so,
She replied, "Don't you know?,
I can't find a towel any place!"

Try writing a limerick of your own in the space provided. Share your limericks with the class.

_____
(title)

_____

_____

_____

_____

_____

_____

_____

_____

Movie Frames

Students can recreate, extend, or change a part of one of the books in this unit by making movie frames that incorporate their writing ideas and illustrations. The construction of the movie frame is simple. Movie frames can be adapted to almost any writing situation in which a story or sequence of events is represented.

To begin your movie frames, establish the writing situation as you focus students' attention on part of a book from this unit. For example, you and your students may decide to write and illustrate a story called "The One Who Got Away on the Chocolate River" as an extension writing activity for *The Chocolate Touch*. Or, students could write and illustrate the sequence of events at the chocolate factory in *Charlie and the Chocolate Factory*.

Follow the directions below to prepare and customize the movie frames.

Materials: 7" x 9" (18 cm x 23 cm) tagboard; construction paper; scissors; crayons, colored pencils, chalks, or markers; masking tape or transparent tape; ruler

Directions

1. Place construction paper lengthwise and cut strips to a height of 7" (18 cm) to use with the frame pattern described below.

2. After students have written their stories, have them decide how the story should be broken into parts and illustrated on each frame. Determine how many frames will be needed to complete the story frames.

3. Have students mark and draw a line every 5" (13 cm) along the length of the construction paper strip to form the frames. Tape strips together as needed for additional frames.

4. Have students write the text and add illustrations for each frame.

5. To open the frame for insertion of the story frames, cut a 7" (18 cm) slit 1" (2.5 cm) in from each 9" (23 cm) length of the tagboard frame. (This will leave 1"/2.5 cm uncut at each end of the slit.)

Have students slide the frame over each story page to create their own "movies."

Cooperative Story Creations

Teacher's Guide

The oral language activity presented below and on pages 45-46 allows students to work in cooperative groups as they create stories based on a set of story components (character, setting, plot). Use the following materials and procedure with the "Cooperative Story Creations" activity.

Materials: character, setting, and plot/problem cards (pages 44-46), reproduced on construction or index paper; scissors; three small containers for holding each set of cards

Procedure

1. Place all character cards (marked "C") in one container, all plot or problem cards (marked "P") in another container, and all setting cards (marked "S") in a third container.

2. Set up cooperative groups of three students. As a "warm-up" activity, let each group choose one card—either a character, setting, or a plot card. Allow the groups to create a story around the card drawn to share with the class. Assign a number to each member in the group (1, 2, or 3). All "ones" draw a character card, all "twos" draw a setting card, and all "threes" draw a plot or problem card.

3. Allow 5-10 minutes for the groups to create a story involving the plot, character, and setting cards they drew. Student groups should present their story creations informally to the class. At the beginning of each story presentation (or dramatization), groups should explain which cards were drawn to give the audience an opportunity to listen for the character, setting, and problem to be solved.

Merry-Go-Round at an amusement park in England [S]	an underground tourist attraction [S]	small town library [S]
movie theater in New York 20th century [S]	6 year-old child's birthday party [S]	Porsche car lot [S]

Cooperative Story Creations *(cont.)*

at the top of Pike's Peak **S**	fifty feet (15m) below the frozen surface of Antarctica **S**	chocolate factory in 2524 A.D. **S**
restaurant on a space station which only serves chocolate dishes **S**	Strange, green curly hairs are growing out of the townspeople's noses. **P**	All four tires on the school bus have melted and are sticking to the pavement. **P**
A large python has escaped from the local zoo. **P**	An antique tractor in a Kansas wheat field disappears. **P**	Twenty-four empty candy wrappers are found near a broken store window. **P**
Music is constantly heard from an abandoned music store. **P**	Trains are using roller blades instead of railroad tracks. **P**	Sunsets have been mysteriously displaying glitter colors. **P**

Cooperative Story Creations *(cont.)*

Every army uniform has been dyed pink.

P

Teachers at an elementary school have begun to speak uncontrollably like cartoon characters.

P

a near-sighted doctor

C

a giant ant with a broken antennae

C

a rock star

C

a dancing grandmother with purple hair

C

an alien with 5 ears

C

a dentist with no teeth

C

ninety-five year-old Karate champion

C

a 3-legged dog

C

an experienced chef

C

telephone operator with the hiccups

C

46

Chocolate Treats Logic Puzzle

Chocolate Club members Greg, Chuck, Yuan, Brigette, and Manuela brought their favorite treats to the club meeting. The treats were R&Z Candies, Zippets Bars, Choco Doodles, Coco Creepies, and Happies. Which club member brought which treat?

Activity

Solve this logic puzzle by using the following information. Place an X in the box to match each club member with his/her treat.

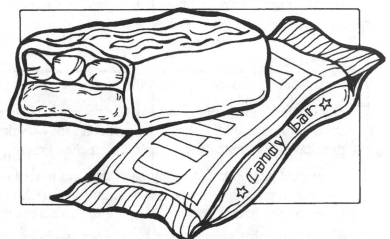

1. Manuela didn't like R&Z candies but really couldn't stand Zippets.

2. Brigette and Greg liked either ChocoDoodles, Coco Creepies, or Happies.

3. Chuck liked R&Z candies more than Yuan did.

4. Greg liked Happies less than Coco Creepies.

5. Brigette loved Coco Creepies.

Treat	Greg	Chuck	Yuan	Brigette	Manuela
R&Z Candies					
Zippets Bars					
Choco Doodles					
Coco Creepies					
Happies					

Logic Challenger: Create your own logic puzzle using the activity above as a model. Have other students try to solve your "Chocolate Treats Logic Puzzle."

Candy Calculations

Teacher's Guide

The activities on pages 49-50 provide students with practice in the following skills: *predicting; recording data; graphing; identifying mean, median,* and *mode.* Use the following materials and suggestions for presenting the activities.

Activity 1 *(Use with page 49.)*

Materials: packages of multi-colored, candy coated chocolate pieces (approximately 47 gram size); page 49, reproduced (See "Procedure" below.); pencils

Procedure

1. Form student groups based on the number of packages. Give each group one full package of candy.

2. Distribute a copy of page 49 to each student. Have students predict how many pieces of candy, the candy colors and how many of each color they think are in the package. Ask them to record their predictions on page 49 and to complete the "Prediction" bar graph using their data.

3. Have students open the candy packages and record on page 49 the actual count for: number of candies in package; candy colors; number of each color. Ask students to complete the bar graph based on the actual results. Compare the actual results to the responses in the prediction column.

   HINT: Students should color bars in the labeled color they indicated on the bottom of the bar graphs. This visually helps students with the comparisons.

Activity 2 *(Use with page 50.)*

Materials: pencils; recorded data from Activity 1; page 50, reproduced for each student

Procedure

1. Use the same grouping of students as in Activity 1. Distribute page 50. Have students record onto their activity sheets each group's actual number of candies in the package. Ask them to use the information to complete the line graph.

   Hint: Point out to students that in a line graph the intersection of the lines is the marking point, not the space between lines as in a bar graph. Then "connecting the dots" as they proceed avoids any problems with the line being formed incorrectly.

2. Present (or review) the steps for finding the average (mean), median, and mode. Use the group information presented in problem #1 on page 50 to find the mean, median, and mode for the number of candies in the packages. Have students complete page 50.

Extension

Predictions using nut-filled, color-coated candies in similar size packages will allow students to form comparisons between product ingredients, amount available, and price. As students make predictions, discuss the following questions: Are there more or less candies in a package of nut-filled candies?, Is the package size the same?, Is the price the same?, Are the colors the same?

Candy Calculations— Predicting and Recording

Prediction   **Actual**

in package_____   # in package_____

Colors	# of each color

Colors	# of each color

16
15
14
13
12
11
10
9
8
7
6
5
4
3
2
1
0

Predicted Colors

16
15
14
13
12
11
10
9
8
7
6
5
4
3
2
1
0

Actual Colors

Candy Calculations— Mean, Median, & Mode

1. Record each group's actual number of candies in the package.

Group 1 _____   **Group 5** _____

Group 2 _____   **Group 6** _____

Group 3 _____   **Group 7** _____

Group 4 _____   **Group 8** _____

2. Form a line graph displaying the actual number in each package.

# of candies: 60 50 40 30 20 10 0

Groups

3. Find the total in problem 1. Divide the total by how many groups were represented. The quotient is the AVERAGE (MEAN) number of candies in the groups' packages.

What is the MEAN (average) number of candies? _____

4. Arrange the answers in problem 1 (actual number of candies in each group's package) in order from least to greatest. The number in the middle of the range is the MEDIAN.

What is the median? _____

5. Look at the answers in problem 1. If any numbers occur more than once, the number occurring most frequently is the MODE.

What is the mode for the group? _____

About Those Candy-Covered Chocolates

A favorite candy of young and old alike is the candy-covered chocolate. The rainbow of bright colors makes them look as good as they taste.

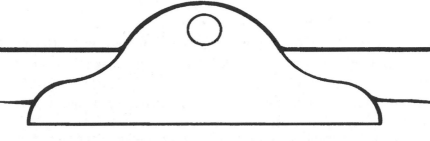

Activity

Try the following candy test to remove the color coating from the candy and reveal the pigment (coloring matter) that was used to produce each color.

Materials: four colors of candy-coated chocolate; about five or six candies of each color; four plastic saucers; water; eye dropper; light-colored blotting paper, cut into four 1" x 5" (2.5 cm x 13 cm) strips

Procedure

1. Place five or six candies of the same color in each plastic saucer.

2. Use an eye dropper to add several drops of water to each saucer.

3. Move the candies around a little in the saucer and turn them over. The color should begin to come off the candies and color the water.

4. Place a strip of blotting paper in each of the saucers so that one end is resting in the colored water, and observe what happens.

Write your observations here:

_____

_____

_____

_____

_____

Classifying Fingerprints

Teacher's Guide

Mr. Wonka could have used a technique for lifting fingerprints to identify the spies who tried to steal his secret recipes. The following fingerprint activity introduces students to some basic fingerprinting techniques as they investigate each other's prints and try to identify a mystery student's fingerprints.

How To Lift Fingerprints

Fingerprints that are left behind on objects are called latent fingerprints. The word latent means "hidden", since these fingerprints are nearly invisible. You can make these prints visible by sprinkling one of two powders. Use talcum powder if the fingerprint is on a hard dark-colored surface. If the fingerprint is on a hard surface that is light-colored, use graphite powder.

Materials: talcum powder or graphite powder; ³/₄" (1.9 cm) wide clear tape; a soft feather; table of items from which to lift fingerprints (Wipe clean of prints before using.); fingerprint cards, page 53 (one per student); large, clean (free of prints) jar, labeled "Mr. Wonka's Secret Recipe Jar"

Directions

1. Shake out a very small amount of powder next to the fingerprint.

2. Dust the powder lightly back and forth over the fingerprint with a soft feather.

3. Brush softly and lightly until every detail of the print is clear.

4. Blow lightly across the print to remove the excess powder.

5. Position tape over the print. Lower it down until it rests on top of the print. Gently smooth it down.

6. Pick up the tape by one corner, lifting the fingerprint with it.

7. Place the tape on black paper if talcum was used, and on white paper if graphite was used.

Have each student place the lifted fingerprints of his/her right hand on the classification card on page 53. The cards can then be used for the following activity.

Fingerprint Identification Activity

Divide the class into 4 groups. Arrange the objects on the table into four groups, matching the number of objects to the number of students in each group. Have each student grab an object firmly, leaving a set of fingerprints on that object. Have each group member return the object to the appropriate section of the table. Group 1 opposes group 2, and group 3 opposes 4. The groups try to match their opponent's fingerprint cards with the objects. The first groups to identify all the opponents' fingerprints win. (For identification purposes use the prepared Fingerprint Classification Cards from page 53.) The winners get to identify the fingerprints on "Mr. Wonka's Secret Recipe Jar." (Teacher needs to have obtained a student's prints prior to the activity.)

Classifying Fingerprints

Look at the tips of your fingers. Notice the tiny lines. The lines on the fingertips form patterns. These fingertip patterns are your fingerprints. No one else in the world has patterns exactly like yours. The fingerprint patterns grow larger as your fingers grow, but their shapes and patterns never change.

The police and the F.B.I. group all fingerprint patterns into these categories: *whorls,* which go in swirls or circles; *loops,* which have a single upside-down U shape; and *arches,* which are shaped like a hill or pencil point.

Eight Types of Patterns

Arches (about 5% of all fingerprints)   ### Loops (about 65% of all prints)

plain
(shaped like a low, rounded hill)

tented
(shaped like a high, pointed tent)

ulnar
(slants toward the little finger side of the hand)

radial
(loop slants toward the thumb side of the hand)

Whorls (about 30% of all prints)

plain whorl
(a pattern in circles or ovals)

central loop pocket
(looks like a whorl tucked inside a loop)

double loop
(S shape)

accidental whorl
(odd patterns, may contain 2 or more of the other patterns)

Fingerprint Classification Cards

Follow your teacher's directions for lifting your fingerprints and placing them on the classification card below. Try classifying the patterns on your own fingers. Use a magnifying lens to help you see the ridges on your fingertips. Look at them carefully. Record the pattern of each one. Complete your Fingerprint Classification Card.

Fingerprint Classification Card

Name _____ Date _____

Thumb	Index	Middle	Ring	Little

Type of pattern _____

Print taken from (item)_____

Taken by _____

Candy and Nutrition

According to the United States Department of Agriculture (USDA), an average 10 year-old child should consume about 2,400 calories per day. However, a child's stomach can only hold enough food from 3 regular meals for about 1,800 calories. That means the additional 600 calories may come from snacking.

The chart shows the percentage provided of the U.S. Recommended Daily Allowance (RDA) of some nutrients. The daily goal is to eat foods in the right amount and right combinations to get 100% of the U.S. RDA of the key nutrients.

Collect the nutritional information labels from the wrappers of 5 candy snacks. Record the name of the item and the nutritional information (if available) in the chart. Use the completed chart information to answer the questions at the bottom of the page. Write your answers on the back of this page.

Snack Item	Percentage of Nutrient							
	Protein	Vitamins A	C	Thiamine	Riboflavin	Niacin	Calcium	Iron
Apple		2	10	2	*	*	*	2
Raisins (1/4 cup/50 mL)	2	*	2	4	2	*	2	6
Potato Chips (1 oz./30 g)	2	*	20	4	2	6	*	2
Pretzels (1 oz./50 mL)	4	*	*	6	4	6	*	2
Carrot (raw)	*	155	10	2	2	2	*	2

indicates information not available

1. Which 5 snacks provide the best variety of the nutrients listed?

2. Why are raisins a better snack than one of the candy items?

3. Are more nutrients provided in potato chips than in one of the first five items?

4. Iron helps form hemoglobin, the red substance in the blood that carries oxygen to body tissues. Which snack provides the most iron?

5. Protein is essential for building, maintaining, and repairing body tissues. Which candies listed provide the most protein?

6. Vitamin C helps maintain healthy blood vessels and aids in the healing process. Which snacks are better in providing Vitamin C?

7. Vitamin A is needed for normal growth, healthy skin, and better vision in dim light. Which snack is the best snack for Vitamin A?

54

The "Scoop" on Chocolate

Chocolate has been around for a very long time. Chocolate is made from the seeds of the cacao (kuh-KOW) tree. The seeds grow inside a pod and are called cacao beans. (English speaking countries refer to them as cocoa beans as a result of early importers misspelling cacao.) The history of chocolate is fascinating. Read the following information about where and how chocolate has been used over the centuries.

Use the map on page 56 to trace the progression of chocolate through the countries beginning with Mexico.

Hernan Cortés (also known as Hernando Cortéz) learned that the Aztecs in Mexico mixed ground, roasted cacao beans with hot water, vanilla, and pepper. In 1528, Cortés took the bitter drink to Spain, but it wasn't well received until the Spaniards added sugar.

The Spanish tried to keep the techniques a secret, but a person from Florence finally was able to take the recipe to Italy where cacao beans were introduced in 1606. They were also introduced in France when chocolate (sho-co-LAY), as the French called it, was taken to France in 1615 for a royal wedding.

Cocoa became a popular beverage in England by 1707 with the addition of milk. It became so popular that the alcohol makers tried to have legislation passed in 1763 to prevent the chocolate drink from being manufactured. Two years later, an English chocolate maker established the first U.S. chocolate factory.

In 1847, Fry & Sons from England developed a method of producing chocolate in a solid form. However, Daniel Peter from Switzerland was given credit in 1874 for first eating chocolate since he improved the Fry & Sons process.

The "Scoop" on Chocolate *(cont.)*

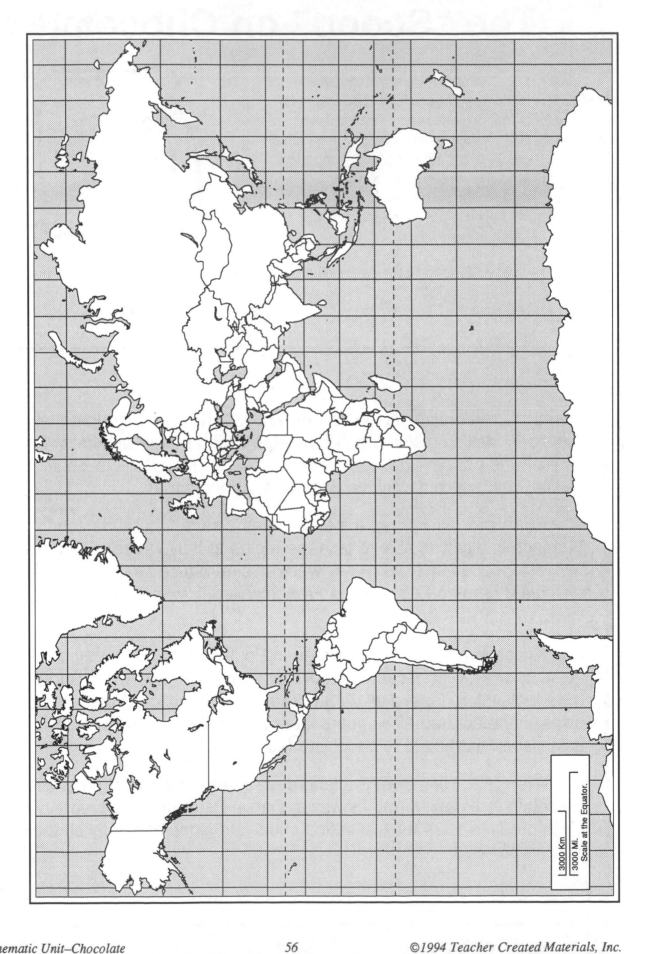

3000 Km
3000 Mi.
Scale at the Equator.

Chocolate Consumers of the World

There are chocolate lovers all over the world! Listed below are some of the major chocolate consuming countries of the world. Beside each country is the average number of pounds/kilograms (lbs/kg) of chocolate eaten per person each year. (Metric conversions, rounded to the nearest tenth, are listed for those using metric measurement.)

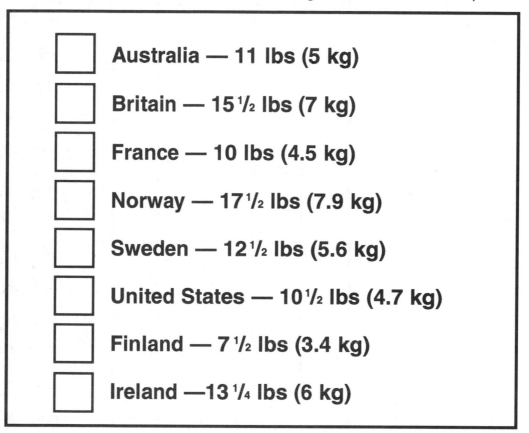

Australia — 11 lbs (5 kg)

Britain — 15 ½ lbs (7 kg)

France — 10 lbs (4.5 kg)

Norway — 17 ½ lbs (7.9 kg)

Sweden — 12 ½ lbs (5.6 kg)

United States — 10 ½ lbs (4.7 kg)

Finland — 7 ½ lbs (3.4 kg)

Ireland —13 ¼ lbs (6 kg)

Activity

A pictograph is a graph in which pictures or symbols represent information. The graph's key shows the value that each symbol or picture represents. The key on page 58 indicates that one chocolate candy symbol represents one pound of chocolate for each person in a year. Create a pictograph on the "Chocolate Consumers of the World" chart on page 58.

Directions

1. Arrange the countries in order from 1-8, with 1 representing the country that consumes the most chocolate and 8 representing the country with the least amount of chocolate consumed. Write the order in the boxes above. Copy the countries (in order) on the chart on page 58.

2. Cut out the correct number of candies from page 58 to represent each country's chocolate consumption. (Use the key to determine how many chocolates to cut out.)

3. Complete the pictograph by gluing the correct number of chocolates next to each country. (Be sure to use half of a chocolate to represent ½ pound, one quarter of a chocolate to show ¼ of a pound, etc. Do the same for kilogram results.)

Chocolate Consumers of the World *(cont.)*

Country	Consumption*						

* Each candy represents 1 pound (.45 kg) per person per year

Exporting Ingredients

Teacher's Guide

The following activity is an extension of the Chocolate Checkers game on pages 13-15. To begin the activity, have students keep the captured ingredient checkers listed below. Provide reference materials for students to use as they research to find some of the countries that export the ingredients labeled on their checkers. Reproduce page 60 and have students complete the ingredients and countries in the appropriate boxes. Using the information gathered, have students label the countries and complete the color key for the map on page 61.

Possible answers for leading exporting countries:

CACAO BEANS
Brazil
Ghana
Ivory Coast
Malaysia
Mexico
Nigeria

SUGAR
Brazil
China
Cuba
France
India
Mexico

COCONUTS
India
Indonesia
Mexico
Philippines
Vietnam

PEANUTS
China
India
U.S.

CASHEWS
Brazil
India

VANILLA
Comoros
Indonesia
Madagascar
Mexico

BANANAS
Brazil
Ecuador
India
Philippines
Uganda

PALM OIL
Malaysia

RAISINS
Australia
Greece
Iran
Turkey

Latitude and Longitude Locations for Exporting Countries

You may find the information provided below useful if you wish to provide student practice in locating countries by using latitude and longitude coordinates. Have students round the degrees first.
(Note: Latitude/longitude lines for the map on page 61 represent 30° reference points. You may wish to have the students mark them before locating countries.)

Australia 30° S - 140° E
Brazil 10° S - 50° W
China 30° N - 110° E
Comoros 13° S - 43° E
Cuba 23° N - 80° W
Ecuador 0° - 80° W
France 45° N - 1° E
Greece 40° N - 22° E
India 20° N - 80° E
Indonesia 0° S - 115° E
Iran 35° N - 55° E

Ivory Coast 8° N - 5° W
Madagascar 20° S - 45° E
Malaysia 5° N - 115° E
Mexico 25° N - 100° W
Nigeria 10° N - 10° E
Philippines 10° N - 125° E
Turkey 40 N° - 40° E
U.S. 40° N - 100° W
Uganda 2° N - 33° E
Vietnam 22° N - 105° E

Exporting Ingredients

Play the Chocolate Checkers Game on pages 13-15. In the boxes below, fill in the names of the ingredients checkers you captured. Research to find out which countries export those items. List the country choices in the appropriate boxes. Use the information from this page to complete the map activity on page 61.

Ingredient
Countries
_____
_____
_____
_____

Ingredient
Countries
_____
_____
_____
_____

Ingredient
Countries
_____
_____
_____
_____

Ingredient
Countries
_____
_____
_____
_____

Ingredient
Countries
_____
_____
_____
_____

Ingredient
Countries
_____
_____
_____
_____

Ingredient
Countries
_____
_____
_____
_____

Ingredient
Countries
_____
_____
_____
_____

Ingredient
Countries
_____
_____
_____
_____

Exporting Ingredients *(cont.)*

On the map, outline and label the countries exporting ingredients you wish to obtain. Color each box in the ingredient key with a different color. Then, color each country you have chosen with the corresponding color that represents the ingredient in the key.

Key

- cacao beans
- almonds
- bananas
- raisins
- sugar
- coconuts
- cashews
- vanilla
- peanuts
- palm oil

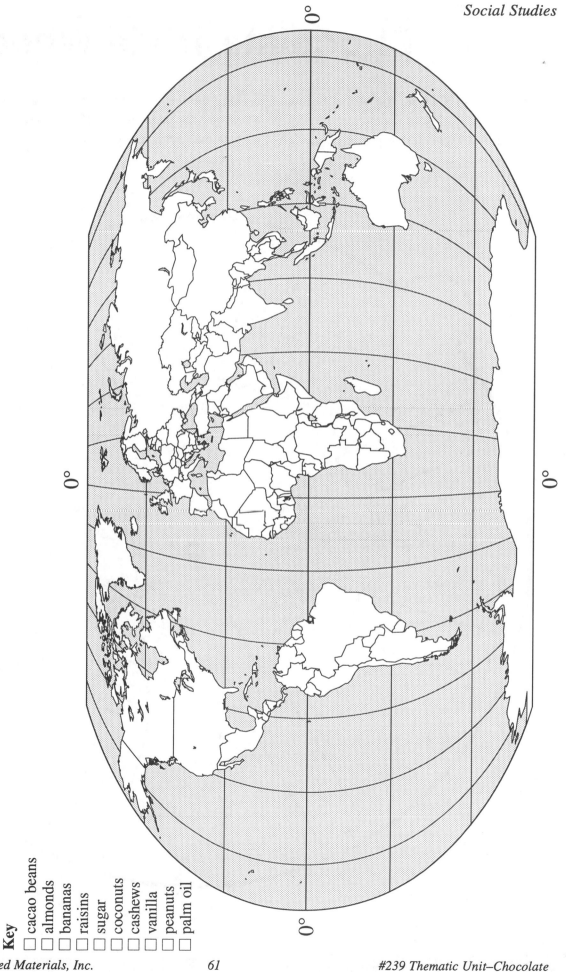

0°

0°

0°

0°

Chocolate Trivia Wheel

Directions: Cut out the wheel below. Cut along the dashed lines to form openings. Cut out the wheel on page 63. Use a fastener to attach the wheel on this page on top of the wheel from page 63. To operate the wheel, grasp one of the tabs and turn the top wheel gently until a match is made.

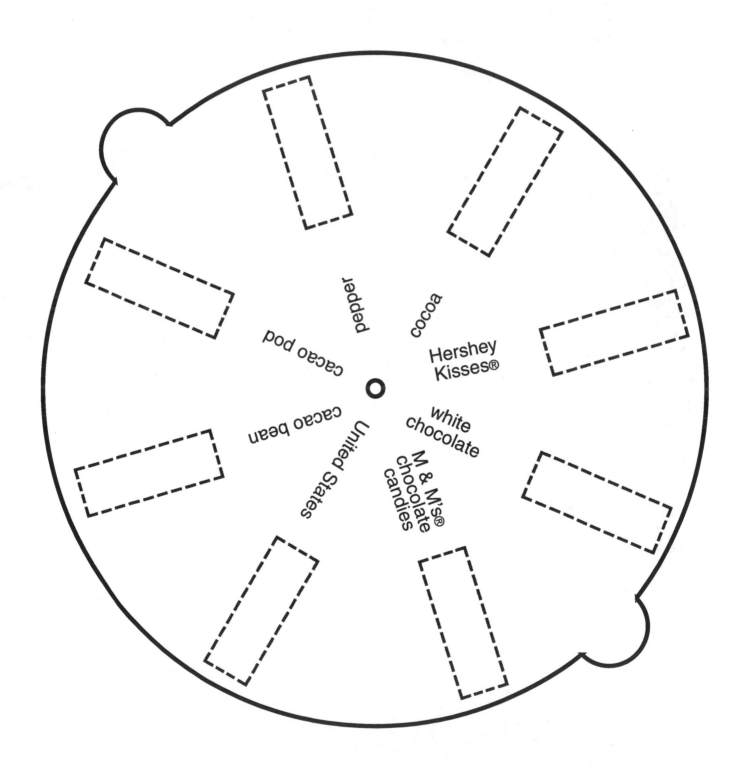

Chocolate Trivia Wheel *(cont.)*

See page 62 for directions and suggestions.

the #1 purchaser
of cacao beans

contains the natural
fat, cocoa butter

contains 25-50
beans

used in cosmetics, soap,
and suntan lotion

no red ones produced
from 1976-1987

added by Aztecs to
flavor chocolate

has cocoa butter but
not cocoa powder

20-25 million made
in one day

Designing a Candy Wrapper

We enjoy the flavor of creamy chocolate, chewy caramel, or sticky taffy. As much as we love the taste of these confections, we often buy them because of their wrappers. Candy comes packaged in a variety of ways—individually wrapped, boxed, or bagged, each with the name of the candy emblazoned somewhere for all to see. Packaging plays a large part in determining the candy we eat.

Let children find out more about candy wrappers and design one of their own. First have them choose their favorite type of candy. Is it maple or toffee, chocolate or mocha creme? What would they call their candy? Once this is done, let them design the packaging for their candy.

Set the stage for this activity by talking about the different types of candy. Ask some of the following questions and chart the children's responses on the board, chart paper, or on an overhead. Set your chart up like this:

Favorites	Types	Ingredients	Packaging

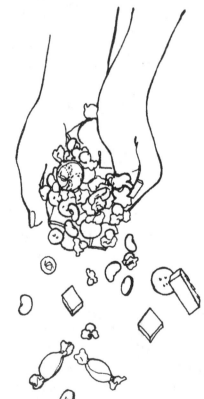

Begin by having students give you the names of their favorites. Next, go through the list with the students. Talk about the types of chocolate and other candy products they chose. Are they pure chocolate, chewy, hard, soft, or filled with nuts and other ingredients? What type of ingredients do they contain—caramel, peanuts, raisins, sugar, butter? Ask them where they can locate this information. Discuss the packaging of the product. Is it bagged, boxed, double wrapped, or individually wrapped and then bagged?

Have students bring in empty candy bar wrappers, boxes, or bags to share. Discuss the location and design of the product name on the wrapper, and where and how the ingredients are listed. Talk about any other information that might be available on the wrapper, such as the size of the candy bar and the nutritional breakdown. (Size, weight, and nutritional information can be used as a springboard for science and math investigations.)

Students are now ready to design their own chocolate candy packaging. (You may wish to have students design wrappers for other types of candy as well as chocolate candies.) Have each student decide the type of candy for which he or she will design a wrapper and create an original name for the product. Then, depending on the candy chosen, have students select the type of wrapper they would like to use: fold-around, box, or bag. (Patterns and directions are provided on pages 65, 66, and 67.)

Have students share their wrappers with the class. Display the candy wrappers on a classroom bulletin board titled, "Creative Candy Wrappers", or, "That's a Wrap!".

Candy Wrapper Patterns

Reproduce the pattern below. Have students cut out the pattern and fold along the dashed lines. Have students design the candy packaging of their choice. Each wrapper should include the name of the candy, the ingredients, and some kind of design.

Candy Wrapper Patterns *(cont.)*

Reproduce the bag onto index paper. Have students add their wrapper information and decorate the wrapper.

NOTE: This pattern may also be used to make shape books into which students can incorporate their poems, stories, and other writing activities from the unit.

66

Candy Box Pattern

Follow the directions below to make a candy box. Candy boxes can be used by students throughout the unit for storage of note cards, game pieces, idea cards, etc. Be sure to include the name of the candy, the ingredients, and some kind of design on the outside of the completed box.

Materials: one each, 9" (23 cm) and 8 ¾" (22 cm) square of construction or index paper; scissors; art materials for decorating and labeling completed box

Directions

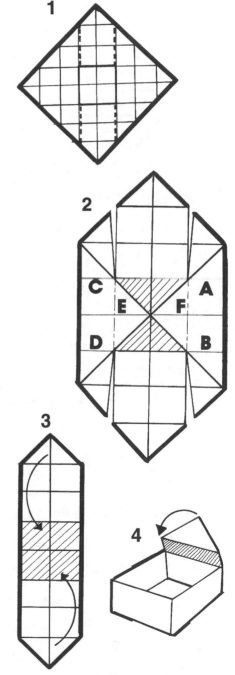

1. Place one of the squares on the table so that one of its corners is pointing towards you. Fold that corner up to the top corner and crease the paper. Unfold the paper and fold the left corner over to the right corner, creasing the paper.

2. Fold the top and bottom corner into the center point. Unfold.

3. Fold the bottom corner up to the fold nearest the top corner. Unfold. Fold the top corner down to the fold nearest the bottom corner. Unfold.

4. Fold the top and bottom corners down to the fold closest to each, respectively. Unfold.

5. Repeat steps 2-4 with the left and right corners.

6. Cut in two squares on each of the fold lines just to the left and right of the bottom corner. Repeat with the top corner. (See illustration 1.)

7. Fold the left corner over along the second vertical fold line and again along the third. Do the same with the right corner. The final folds should be along lines E and F. (See illustration 2.)

8. Fold A and B inward so that they point up (to serve as tabs). Do the same with the fold lines C and D. (See illustration 2.)

9. Fold the left and right sides up, overlapping the flaps of each. This forms a box shape in the center.

10. Fold the bottom corner up and over the edge of the box so that the point of the corner rests in the center of the box. (See illustrations 3 and 4.) Repeat this procedure with the top flap.

Repeat the entire process with the second square. Place one inside the other to create a box.

Chocolate Consumption Survey

For one week, record each time you eat anything that contains chocolate or cocoa. List the items in the appropriate categories. Then, answer the questions at the bottom of the page.

Day	Breakfast	Lunch	Dinner	Snack
Sunday				
Monday				
Tuesday				
Wednesday				
Thursday				
Friday				
Saturday				
Subtotal				

Add all subtotals for a final total. Record the final total here: _____

1. If you eat chocolate at about the same rate all year, what do you think your average monthly chocolate consumption will be? _____

2. Based on the information above, what do you estimate your average yearly chocolate consumption to be? _____

A Closer Look at Snacks

Good News For Kids!

Researchers report that chocolate contains compounds that slow down tooth decay and inhibit plaque buildup. Fat is thought to interfere with bacteria while calcium protects the enamel. Yet another protective substance, called casein, has been found in chocolate which is a milk protein and cavity fighter.

Scientific tests prove that chocolate neither causes nor aggravates acne.

Good News For Adults!

For people with heart trouble there is a heart stimulant called theobromine which is found naturally in the cacao bean.

Chocolate is almost salt and cholesterol free, although some of the ingredients added to chocolate products may not be.

Snack Time!

The snacks below and on page 70 are fun to make and eat. It is important to remember that people of all ages should eat chocolate and other candy items in moderation.

No Bake Cookies

Ingredients

2 cups (500 mL)sugar
1 teaspoon (5 mL) vanilla
1/2 cup (125 mL) cocoa

1/2 cup (125 mL) peanut butter
1/2 cup (125 mL) milk
1/2 cup (125 mL) margarine
3 cups (750 mL) quick-cooking oatmeal

Directions

1. Mix the sugar and cocoa in a pan. Add the milk and margarine.
2. Put the pan on medium heat and cook until it starts to boil. Remove from heat.
3. Add the vanilla, peanut butter, and quick-cooking oatmeal. Stir thoroughly.
4. Drop spoonfuls onto waxed paper. Allow cookies to cool before eating.

A Closer Look at Snacks *(cont.)*

The recipes below are quick and easy to prepare. You may either choose a recipe to make at home on your own, or work in groups in class to make a favorite recipe.

Cocoa

Try some homemade cocoa for a real treat. Hot cocoa served with homemade cookies or chocolate pie is "lip-smacking" good!

Directions: In a saucepan, mix $1/3$ cup (80 mL) of sugar, $1/3$ cup (80 mL) of cocoa powder, and $1/4$ teaspoon (1 mL) of salt. Add $1\,1/2$ cups (375 mL) of water. Stir constantly and bring the mixture to a boil. Stir and boil an additional 2 minutes. Stir in $4\,1/2$ cups (about 1 L) of milk. Heat the liquid but do not boil. Add $1/4$ teaspoon (1 mL) of vanilla. Just before serving the cocoa, use an egg beater or wire whisk to stir the chocolate and make it foamy. Add a marshmallow or dollop of whipped cream.

Chocolate "Spider" Treats

Don't let the name fool you! These spidery-looking treats are delicious. Try them and see for yourself.

To make your Chocolate "Spider" Treats you will need: 8 ounce (180 g) milk chocolate bar, 2 cups (about 500 mL) crisp rice cereal, and $1/2$ cup (about 125 mL) shredded coconut.

Directions: Melt the chocolate in a double boiler. As an alternative, use a microwave oven for 1-2 minutes at about 50% power. Stir in the rice cereal and coconut. Drop the mixture onto waxed paper, a teaspoonful at a time. Chill the mixture in refrigerator until the mixture is set. (Makes about 2 dozen.)

Easy-to-Make Chocolate Pie

To make this simple recipe, use a prepared graham cracker pie crust. Prepare instant chocolate pudding according to the package directions. Pour the pudding into the pie shell. Top with a ready-made whipped cream. Serve and enjoy!

70

Chocolate Town

One of the most successful stories in the chocolate business has been that of the Hershey Company®. Originally built in 1903 by founder Milton Hershey, the chocolate factory is just one facet of this amazing town. Workers' homes, parks, a zoo, a golf course, a football field, an outdoor theater, a hotel, a museum, and even a home for orphan children are just a few of the amenities to be found here. Streets are named as reminders of the chocolate industry—Cocoa, Trinidad, and Chocolate are some. Street lights are even shaped like chocolate kisses. It is the ultimate chocolate town! Have the students read about Hershey, especially the fascinating biography *Milton Hershey, Chocolate King* by Mary Malone (Garrard Publishing Company, 1971). Divide the students into groups and have each design a chocolate town. Listed below and on pages 72 and 73 are some elements you may want them to include in their projects.

Research

There are a number of familiar and popular names in the chocolate industry besides Hershey®. Some of them are Mars®, Ghiradelli®, Godiva®, Whitman®, Brach®, Nestle®, Tobler®, and Cadbury®. Instruct the students to find out more information about two of these companies. (Look for mailing addresses on the candy wrappers or boxes. Some addresses are provided on page 80.)

Products

The list of chocolate goodies is endless. There are chocolate chip cookies, chocolate mint ice cream, chocolate mousse, chocolate fondue, chocolate soufflé, chocolate bonbons, chocolate truffles, and even chocolate pancakes! Have the groups determine what kind of chocolate confection they want their town to manufacture.

Recipes

Direct the students to find a recipe for the chocolate product they have chosen. If it is a new invention they will have to create their own original recipe. There are numerous chocolate cookbooks on the market. Three books not to be overlooked are *Chocolate, the Consuming Passion* by Sandra Boynton (Workman Publishing, 1982), *The Chocolate Cookbook* by Marcy and Michael Mager (Scholastic Book Services, 1977) and *Chocolate* by Jacqueline Dineen (Carolrhoda Books, 1991).

Chocolate Town *(cont.)*

Brainstorm

After deciding on the type of chocolate their town is going to produce, have each group determine an appropriate chocolate name for the town. The chocolate can be in any form that already exists or one that they have invented. Within each group students should brainstorm a list of the types of town buildings they want to include.

Models

Make a three-dimensional town using cylindrical oatmeal boxes, cereal boxes, shoe boxes, and other clean, empty containers. Cut a sheet of heavy cardboard from a moving box and paint one side black with tempera or spray paint. Cover the boxes with construction paper or paint. Add details such as doors and windows. Paint streets, railroads, etc., onto the dry base. When all the pieces are dry, arrange them on the cardboard base. Glue or tape them in place. Name and label the streets and buildings. If preferred, groups can make a mural or map of their town on a large sheet of butcher paper. Drawings should include the chocolate factory, houses, parks, library, and other structures.

Advertising

Have the students create an ad campaign for the candy that they're manufacturing in their town. They will need to design a wrapper with a logo and art work. A snappy slogan should be devised to entice people to buy the candy. Advise students that they need to make a container or box for store displays. (See directions for making candy boxes on page 67.)

Chocolate Code

Boxed chocolates are encoded with different notations in their chocolate coverings to designate the different flavors. Share samples of chocolate boxes with the class. Have students create their own notations for their chocolate products.

Posters

The students will need to make posters to advertise their chocolate wares. They can use tagboard or other sheets of heavy paper and any art supplies they would like (e.g., neon colored pens, glitter, colored art tissue, actual candy wrappers, and magazine cut-outs).

Chocolate Town *(cont.)*

Commercials

Direct the students to write a commercial for their chocolate goodies. Have them write a script and make their own props, including an actual sample. When the groups are ready, videotape the commercials. . Present them to the whole class. Determine which ad was most effective and why.

Samples

Provide samples for the public by making scratch and sniff buttons. Cut out shaped pieces (the shape of the chocolate they are manufacturing) from index paper (available at copy shops and computer supply stores). Spread a thin layer of white glue on each shape and immediately sprinkle with cocoa powder (for best results, pre-sift cocoa powder through a hand-sifter onto wax paper) or chocolate drink mix. Roll a strip of masking tape into a circle, sticky side out, and attach it to the back of the paper. Pass out the samples for competitors to wear. (Some students may want to experiment by spraying paper shapes with chocolate extract or finding their own way to create scratch and sniff buttons.)

History

Have the groups write a history of how their chocolate town came into existence. Tell about the founder(s) and how the idea for their chocolate confection came about. For inspiration on inventions, the students might want to read *Steven Caney's Invention Book* by Steven Caney (Workman Publishing, 1985). If the groups would rather write about adventures that their founder(s) had in earlier days, have them read fun novels like *Chocolate Fever* by Robert Kimmel Smith (Dell Publishing, 1972) and *The Chocolate Touch* by Patrick Skene Catling.

Music

Tell the groups to write a song that residents of their town like to sing. (Remind them that this is a chocolate-based economy.) The groups can record their songs on video or a tape recorder. Share all songs with the rest of the class.

Display

Each day, plan for a different group to display its chocolate town and projects. Have them give oral reports to the rest of the class.

Bulletin Board Suggestions

Reading

Chocolate Book Report

During silent reading time, let a student give an oral book report to the teacher. This allows students practice in oral presentations while providing needed reading time for the other students.

Teachers can request title, author, main characters, setting, and plot during individual oral book reports, simultaneously guiding students in these required areas.

Upon completion of the oral book report, the student is given the chocolate candy pattern to fill out and add to the cookie. A pattern is easily prepared by cutting out the shape of a candy and the student's name, title of book, and the name of the author. Other information about the book may be added, if desired.

At the end of the unit, the student having read the most receives his/her favorite chocolate treat.

Chocolate Box Reading Record

Reproduce page 75 for each student. Make extra copies as the need arises. Prepare the boxes by cutting along the dashed lines and cutting out the chocolate patterns at the bottom of the page. Have each student personalize his or her chocolate box.

As a student completes a book or a required number of pages, he or she writes the book title on a piece of chocolate and adds chocolate to the box by partially inserting it through the dashed line.

Social Studies

Enlarge the world map on page 56. Reproduce the patterns on page 76. Cut and color each. Place the patterns around the world map and connect each product to its major exporting country (or countries) with yarn. The completed bulletin board can be used with several of the activities throughout the unit.

Poetry

Let students display their "Ode to Chocolate", "Lickable Limericks", or other poems related to the theme on a poetry bulletin board. Use the pattern and directions on page 77 to prepare each poem for display.

Reading Bulletin Board

Decorate and color the border of the chocolate box. Cut slits along the dashed lines in the paper chocolate wrappers. Cut out and insert a piece of candy into a paper wrapper each time you complete a book or the number of pages required by your teacher. Write the book title on the candy.

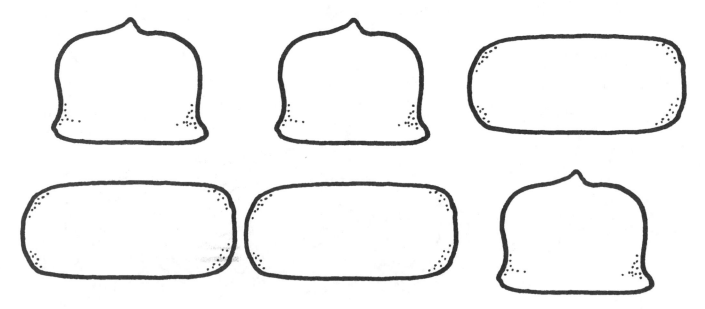

Products for Social Studies
Bulletin Board

cacao beans

vanilla

butter

peanuts

raisins

cashews

oats

bananas

almonds

coconuts

Bulletin Board Patterns for Poetry

Cut out the pattern. Use a black pen or marker to write a poem in the center of the pattern. If desired, shade in the candy pattern lightly with a brown crayon or art pencil. Display your poem on a bulletin board.

Congratulations!

has a real "Sweet Tooth" when it comes
to learning about Chocolate.

What a fine project!

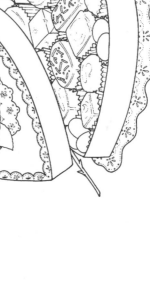

Date

Teacher

78

Answer Key *(cont.)*

Page 16
Activity 1
1. 3; 3/24 or 1/8, 2. 5; 5/24, 3. 2/24 or 1/12
Activity 2
1. a. 2/12 or 1/6, b. 1/12, c. 4/12 or 1/3
2. a. 1/12, b. 3/12 or 1/4, c. 3/12 or 1/4

Page 22
1. Revenue from Sales: $25, $60, $75, $70, $45,
2. $.10, 3. $.30
4.

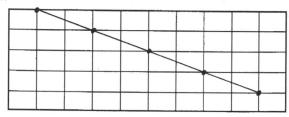

Page 23
1. $.50, 2. $.10, 3. quantity increases 4. quantity decreases

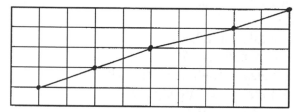

Page 24

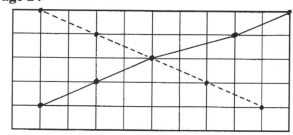

1. $.30
2. There is less demand. People would not buy them.
3. Demand would be greater than supply, creating a shortage.
4. Answers may vary. Accept reasonable, supported responses.

Page 38

Page 39
1. John Hannon, 2. Randolphe Lindt, 3. Milton Hershey, 4. Coenraad van Houten, 5. Hernan Cortes, 6. Montezuma II, 7. James Baker, 8. Henri Nestlé, 9. Jean Tobler, 10. Cadbury

Page 40
1. a. 22 lbs (10 kg)
   b. 2,750,000,000 lbs (1,237,500,000 kg)
2. a. more than 350 cups (79.1 L)/week
   b. 1,550 cups (350.3 L)/month
   c. 14,000 cups (3,164 L) per week
3. a. 750 lbs (337.5 kg)
   b. 10,250 lbs (4612.5 kg)
4. 2000 calories
5. a. 15.24 m
   b. 8 yds.

Page 47
Encourage students to work in groups, discussing the possible treats each club member might choose based on the information in the chart and the process of elimination. For this activity, the teacher should focus on the student's thought process and his or her ability to analyze information in order to arrive at and support a solution.

Page 54
Answers are based on label information. Accept responses supported by chart data.

Page 63
M & M's®— no red ones produced from 1976-1987
United States— the #1 purchaser of cacao beans
cacao pod— contains 20-25 beans
pepper— added by Aztecs to flavor chocolate
Hershey Kisses®— 20-25 million made in one day
white chocolate— has cocoa butter but not cocoa powder
cocoa butter— used in cosmetics, soap, and suntan lotion
cacao bean— contains the natural fat, cocoa butter

Bibliography

Adoff, Arnold. *Chocolate Dreams*. Lothrop, Lee, & Shephard Books, 1989.

Allamand, Pascale. *Cocoa Beans to Daisies*. Frederick Warne and Company, 1978.

Ammon, Richard. *The Kids' Book of Chocolate*. Atheneum, 1987.

Anderson, Marilyn. *Hot Fudge Pickles*. Willowslip Press, 1984.

Boynton, Sandra. *Chocolate, the Consuming Passion*. Workman Publishing, 1982.

Busenberg, Bonnie. *Vanilla, Chocolate, & Strawberry*. Lerner Publishing Company, 1994.

Caney, Steven. *Invention Book*. Workman Publishing, 1985.

Catling, Patrick. *The Chocolate Touch*. Morrow & Company, 1952.

"Chocolate: A User's Manual". *The Mother Earth News*. November/December, 1988, 114:86-88.

"Chocolate: Food of the Gods". *National Geographic*. November, 1984, 166:664-687.

"Chocolate Glossary". *Better Homes & Gardens*. October, 1989, 67:159.

Dahl, Ronald. *Charlie and the Chocolate Factory*. Knopf, 1964.

    Charlie and the Great Glass Elevator. Knopf, 1972.

    Danny the Champion of the World. Knopf, 1975.

    Fantastic Mr. Fox. Knopf, 1970.

    James and the Giant Peach. Knopf, 1964.

    Witches, The. Penguin, 1985.

Dineen, Jacqueline. *Chocolate*. Carolrhoda Books, 1990.

"For Chocolate Lovers". *World Monitor*. February, 1992, 5:10.

Hearn, Michael Patrick, sel. by. *The Chocolate Book*. Caedmon, 1983.

"How Sweet It'll Be". *American Health*. June, 1988, 7:24.

Kourilsky, Marilyn. *Understanding Economics*. Addison-Wesley, 1983.

Loeper, John L. *Mr. Marley's Main Street Confectionery*. Atheneum, 1979.

Mager, March and Michael. *The Chocolate Cookbook*. Scholastic Book Services, 1977.

Malone, Mary. *Milton Hershey Chocolate King*. Garrad Publishing Company, 1977.

Mitgusch, Ali. *From Cocoa Bean to Chocolate*. Carolrhoda Books, 1975.

O'Neill, Catherine. *Let's Visit a Chocolate Factory*. Troll Associates, 1988.

Perl, Lila. *The Great Ancestor Hunt*. Clarion Books, 1989.

Smith, Robert. *Chocolate Fever*. Dell Publishing, 1972.

"Sybaritic to Some". *Smithsonian*. February, 1986, 16:54-60.

Wolfman, Ira. *Do People Grow on Family Trees?*. Workman Publishing, 1991.

Company Addresses

(See page 5 for suggested uses.)
Hershey Chocolate
Hershey, PA 17033-0815

E.J. Brach Corporation
4656 West Kinzie, Chicago, IL 60644
Tootsie Roll Industries, Chicago, IL 60629

Nestlé Chocolate and Confection Company Incorporated
Purchase, NY 10577

Mars Inc./M & M
Hackettstown, NJ 17840

NOTE: Address letters to Attention: Consumer Relations